Education and Natural Disasters

Also available in the Education as a Humanitarian Response Series

Education as a Global Concern, Colin Brock
Education and HIV/AIDS, Nalini Asha Biggs
Education and Minorities, Chris Atkin
Education and Reconciliation, Julia Paulson
Education, Refugees and Asylum Seekers, Lala Demirdjian
Education, Aid and Aid Agencies, Zuki Karpinska

Education and Natural Disasters

Education as a Humanitarian Response

Edited by

David Smawfield

BLOOMSBURY

LONDON · NEW DELHI · NEW YORK · SYDNEY

Bloomsbury Academic
An imprint of Bloomsbury Publishing Plc

50 Bedford Square   175 Fifth Avenue
London   New York
WC1B 3DP   NY 10010
UK   USA

www.bloomsbury.com

First published 2013

© David Smawfield and contributors, 2013

All rights reserved. No part of this publication may be reproduced or transmitted in any form or by any means, electronic or mechanical, including photocopying, recording, or any information storage or retrieval system, without prior permission in writing from the publishers.

David Smawfield and contributors has asserted their right under the Copyright, Designs and Patents Act, 1988, to be identified as Authors of this work.

No responsibility for loss caused to any individual or organization acting on or refraining from action as a result of the material in this publication can be accepted by Bloomsbury Academic or the author.

British Library Cataloguing-in-Publication Data
A catalogue record for this book is available from the British Library.

ISBN: HB: 978-1-4411-9991-1
      PB: 978-1-4411-6699-9
      PDF: 978-1-4411-1838-7
      ePub: 978-1-4411-6513-8

Library of Congress Cataloging-in-Publication Data
A catalog record for this title is available from the Library of Congress.

Typeset by Fakenham Prepress Solutions, Fakenham, Norfolk NR21 8NN
Printed and bound in Great Britain

Contents

Notes on Contributors

Colin Bangay is Senior Education Adviser within the UK's Department for International Development (DFID). He is currently based in the British High Commission, New Delhi, India.

Kevin Beaton is Headteacher at Sidney Smith School, an 11–16 age group mixed comprehensive school in the Hull Local Education Authority, UK.

Colin Brock is Senior Research Fellow at the University of Oxford, UK, and specialises in Comparative and International Education. He holds a UNESCO Chair in the field of Education as a Humanitarian Response.

Robin Burns is Adjunct Associate Professor, in the School of Public Health, La Trobe University, Melbourne, Australia.

Fumiaki Ema is Professor of Education in the Graduate School of Teacher Training, Yamagata University, Japan.

David Ledgard is Headteacher at Cottingham Croxby Primary School, Cottingham, East Yorkshire, England.

Benjamin Newton is Associate Director of Admissions and School Design Associate for Avenues: The World School, New York, USA.

David Smawfield is a Senior International Education Consultant. He has worked in more than twenty countries spanning Europe, Africa, Asia and the Americas.

Zhou Zhong is Associate Professor in the Institute of Education, Tsinghua University, China. She gained her doctorate at the University of Oxford, UK.

Series Editor's Preface

Underlying the entire series on *Education as a Humanitarian Response* is the well-known adage in education: 'if we get it right for those most in need we will probably get it right for all if we take the same approach.' That sentiment was born in relation to those with special educational needs within a full mainstream schooling system. In relation to this series it is taken further to embrace the special educational needs of those facing disadvantage of various kinds, including disasters, whether natural, man-made, or a combination of both. Much of value to the provision of normal mainstream systems can be learned from the holistic approach that necessarily follows in response to disasters. Sadly, very little of this potential value is actually perceived, and even less is embraced. Consequently one of the aims of the series, both in the core volume, *Education as a Global Concern*, and in the contributing volumes, is to bring into the mainstream the notion of education as a humanitarian response, and those seeking to serve it as teachers, other educators and practitioners, administrators and politicians.

The theme of this book *Education and Natural Disasters* is particularly apposite as it is able to describe and discuss the range of contexts of such events and illustrate the human hand in some of them both directly and indirectly. On the other hand its prime concern is to expose and highlight the human response, especially with regard to education. This of course can include relevant education prior to a disaster both in terms of understanding how it comes about and also how to respond to it. So while this theme clearly falls into the category of 'education in emergencies', it also shows how some degree of preparedness through education can improve the response. Such needs and responses are well documented by the Inter-Agency Network for Education in Emergencies (INEE), the leading and coordinating NGO.

Education in all its forms in response to natural disasters is also contributing to the radical thinking about the type of education we need to be fostering in order to be successful in meeting the fundamental challenge of sustaining the human and physical environments on planet Earth.

Colin Brock
UNESCO Chair in Education as a Humanitarian Response, Oxford, UK

Foreword

David Smawfield

What roles can education play in helping to respond to natural disasters, in ameliorating and mitigating them, preparing people how to respond, and even helping to prevent them? To what extent are so-called natural disasters linked to human behaviour and what are the potential and limitations of education to influence or change that behaviour? These are the kinds of question this volume will endeavour to address. It will examine, in international perspective, experiences, know-how, lessons and challenges drawn from natural hazards and disasters of different types and from a range of countries at varied stages of socio-economic development. Following a subject overview by David Smawfield, six country case studies are presented by individual contributors: bushfires in Australia, by Robin Burns; natural hazards in India, by Colin Bangay; Hurricane Katrina in the United States, by Benjamin Newton; floods in Hull and the East Riding, UK, by Kevin Beaton and David Ledgard; earthquake in China, by Zhou Zhong; and earthquake, tsunami and nuclear disaster in Japan, by Fumiaki Ema. A short concluding section will then draw together some key points emerging from all of the above.

Education and Natural Disasters: A Selective Overview

David Smawfield

1

Chapter Outline

Introduction

With a subject as broad as 'education and natural disasters', any attempt to offer a comprehensive overview in just one chapter can only be selective. Nevertheless, an attempt is made here to provide as broad an introduction as possible in relation to some main perspectives, themes and modalities. These include: policy and institutional frameworks; school response; school buildings and safety; education and natural disasters curriculum content and approaches in the school milieu; the role of teachers in disaster response; non-formal and informal education, including public education; the role and contribution of the private sector, including public/private partnerships; further and higher education; and the role of research. An attempt is also made to acknowledge aspects that are not covered here, and where there are information gaps and potential areas for future investigation.

In the researching of this chapter, very interesting patterns, with potential policy implications, were discovered in an analysis of programmes of higher education promoted through a key internet portal. In view of their adjudged importance and possible contribution to knowledge, these patterns are discussed in slightly greater detail compared to other areas examined. Before proceeding with any of the above, however, it will be helpful to take further steps to set the subject context, including reference to terminology and scope.

Setting the Context, Terminology and Scope

A definition for the term 'Natural Disaster' is somewhat elusive. Not all major dictionaries include the phrase. However, *Webster's Online Dictionary*, which claims to be the World's largest dictionary, defines natural disasters as: 'sudden calamitous events producing great material damage, loss and distress. They are the result of natural phenomena such as earthquakes, floods etc.' This is as workable a definition as any and will be assumed as the basic understanding of the term from which to pursue a discussion in rather more depth. However, a rather important semantic position, which should not be ignored, in view of the importance of the source, is that of the United Nations International Strategy for Disaster Reduction (UNISDR). It takes the view that 'there is no such thing as a "natural" disaster, only natural hazards' (UNISDR, 2011b).

Among the more familiar natural hazards, which can lead to 'natural disasters', according to the understanding of the term being developed here, are: avalanche, cold wave, cyclone, drought, earthquake, epidemic, flood, heat wave, insect infestation, land slide, mud flow, storm, storm surge, tornado, tsunami, volcano and wild fire. These are the categorisations for natural hazards used by the United Nations itself. However, even this list is not exhaustive. Other sources will include potential space hazards such as meteoric impact events, solar flares and gamma ray bursts. There are also other more obscure earthly hazards that could be included such as 'limnic eruptions': a rare type of natural disaster in which carbon dioxide or other gases suddenly erupt from deep lake water, suffocating wildlife, livestock and humans. The most notorious event of this kind (and only the second ever recorded) occurred in 1986 in Lake Nyos: a crater lake in the Northwest Region of Cameroon. The eruption asphyxiated over 1,700 people.

In building an understanding of the term 'natural disaster' a stage further, it is important to consider root causes. Those of a religious persuasion might infer an 'act of God'. Even to those without faith, the conventional understanding of a 'natural disaster' has been that it is something 'caused by factors extraneous to man' (Burton and Kates, 1964: 43, quoted in Boehn, 1996: 35). However, as Boehn goes on eloquently to argue, and with which the current writer would agree, the term arguably needs to encompass a newer dimension: man-made natural disasters. The examples Boehn provides include: alpine landslides caused by building too many ski lifts; desertification as a result of too much livestock husbandry, and the consequences of the greenhouse effect caused by emissions of chlorofluorocarbons. In taking this particular stance, it therefore follows that education needs to go beyond acceptance of natural disasters and preparedness, mitigation and response, but must also play a role in natural disaster prevention – especially where root causes can be traced to the behaviour of mankind.

In some definitions of the term 'natural disaster' there need to be significant direct human consequences, such as heavy loss of life and/or destruction and damage of property. However, the loss of coral reefs due to ocean overheating and activities of man, the extinction of animal species or the deaths of millions of seabirds and other marine life as a result of oil spillages, toxic waste disposal and habitat destruction are all disasters *of* and *for* nature. Arguably, such disasters ought also to be embraced by the term 'natural disasters' – especially in the context of this book, where an important consideration is the role that education can play in prevention, mitigation and understanding of the causal relationships that can lead to disasters involving nature and natural forces. In summary, then, it is concluded and accepted here that a 'natural disaster' is something that involves substantial human, economic or environmental loss.

4 Education and Natural Disasters

One of the most important findings that emerge from a review of the literature on natural disasters, especially in view of some of the discussion to follow, is that risks from natural disasters are not spread equally across the globe. Moreover, the impact of such disasters when they do occur is often not shouldered equally by all sections of society. For instance, one proxy indicator of disaster prevalence comprises World Bank statistics cited in Dilley et al. (2005) on emergency loans and reallocation of existing loans to meet disaster reconstruction needs from 1980 through 2003. According to these data:

> total emergency lending and loan reallocation from 1980 through 2003 was $14.4 billion. Of this, $12 billion went to the top 20 countries: India, Turkey, Bangladesh, Mexico, Argentina, Brazil, Poland, Colombia, Iran, Honduras, China, Chile, Zimbabwe, Dominican Republic, El Salvador, Algeria, Ecuador, Mozambique, Philippines and Vietnam.
>
> (Dilley et al., 2005: 23–4)

Cavallo and Noy point out that:

> the overwhelming majority of people affected and killed by natural disasters reside in developing countries, particularly in the Asia-Pacific region. ... 96% of the people killed and 99% of the people affected by natural disasters over the period 1970–2008 were in the Asia-Pacific region, Latin America and the Caribbean, or Africa.
>
> (Cavallo and Noy, 2010: 11)

Research undertaken separately by Toya and Skidmore used 'disaster impact data over time to examine the degree to which the human and economic losses from natural disasters are reduced as economies develop' (Toya and Skidmore, 2007: 1). It found that 'countries with higher income, higher educational attainment, greater openness, more complete financial systems and smaller government experience fewer losses' (ibid.: 1). Crucially, they also point to the fact that educational attainment is one of the key variables inversely correlated with deaths caused by natural disasters (ibid.: 6).

Gitter and Barham examined 'the impact on secondary school attainment in rural Honduras of four key variables affecting household choices: wealth, credit access, crop choice and shocks' (Gitter and Barham, 1999: 1). The shock in question in this particular case study was 'Hurricane Mitch', the most powerful hurricane of the 1998 Atlantic hurricane season, which badly affected Honduras. Their research 'results show directly that credit-rationed households hit by a shock were likely to remove their children from school'. Furthermore, 'credit-constrained households have lower educational attainment and are more likely to be adversely affected by negative shocks' (ibid.: 11).

According to the United Nations Development Programme (UNDP):

> Women, girls, boys and men belonging to different age and socio-economic strata have distinct vulnerabilities, and this shapes the way they experience disaster, and also their ability to recover from it. In countries where gender discrimination is tolerated, women and girls are particularly vulnerable to natural hazards. Not only is the percentage of women and girls who die higher in these countries, but the incidence of gender-based violence – including rape, human trafficking and domestic abuse – is also known to increase exponentially during and after disasters. Most disasters place an undue burden on women and girls who are responsible for unpaid work such as providing care, water and food for households.
>
> (UNDP, 2010: 1)

The same source cites the facts that 'disasters lower women's life expectancy more than men's' and that 'women, boys and girls are 14 times more likely than men to die during a disaster' (ibid.: 2).

With regard to the term 'Education', the same dictionary source quoted above defines the word as: 'the activities of educating or instructing … that impart knowledge or skill'. This broad definition will also be adopted for the purposes of this book. However, in view of what is to follow, it is also helpful to disaggregate some of the more important sub-forms that education can take, including types of activity and modality. Three such crucial sub-terms commonly used are 'formal education', 'non-formal education' and 'informal education'. In terms of further disaggregation, which can cross-cut these last three mentioned terms, it is worth distinguishing between public sector and private sector education; between profit and not-for-profit modalities; and government and non-government approaches – and all of which are again not necessarily mutually exclusive.

It is useful, too, to conceptualise different permutations for transacting education by considering 'who does the learning and who does the teaching?' There are many interesting possibilities. It should not necessarily be assumed that experts have a monopoly of knowledge. For example: indigenous knowledge can be sought, recognised and built upon as part of a disaster risk-reduction strategy. Possibilities of this kind are exemplified in Shaw et al. (2009). Moreover, in the Indian context, it has been demonstrated (AIDMI, 2011) how community-to-community learning can play a role in helping affected communities share their experiences and learn from each other. This Indian example pertains to how experience was shared from Bihar to Tamil Nadu.

'Child-to-child' education has been recognised as a powerful model in many contexts over many years. (See, for example, Child-to-Child Trust, 2011). It has equally great potential in the context of education and natural disasters. However, this modality does appear under-represented among current practical resource literature. For example, no child-to-child themed titles were to be found among the more than 240 'Education and School Safety' related practical resources within the 'Documents and Publications' section of the United Nations *PreventionWeb* site when this was searched in September 2011. One interesting title that did appear there, however, was *Let Our Children Teach Us*. Such a slogan underscores the point that educating children in schools can be a key means of getting appropriate messages and practice relayed to homes and communities. As an interesting example of informal learning, where it is an activity rather than a person that does the 'teaching': educational games have been used successfully in Vietnam and Indonesia to convey messages and engage youth in risk reduction (IFRC, 2010).

There is a danger of thinking of natural disaster-related education programmes as programmes designed entirely on that subject. There is, however, important scope and opportunity to 'mainstream' natural disaster-related subject matter and considerations into almost any context. This happens most obviously, of course, in relation to the school curriculum (as will be discussed in more detail below), where earthquakes and flooding, preparedness and response, for instance, might form part, say, of the teaching of geography. However, there are other less obvious areas of approach. An example of good practice in this regard includes a resource developed by the World Health Organization to integrate emergency preparedness and response into undergraduate nursing curricula (WHO, 2008).

This section of the chapter has illustrated the wide range of differing types of approach to education and learning with regard to natural disasters. All approaches have their contribution to make and it is fairly safe to assume that there is no single best way. Fitness for purpose is likely to be key. However, a final word on the subject of approach is to acknowledge that there can also be benefits of approaches that are holistic in nature, and which combine different and 'multi-pronged' strategies. This is expressly to create synergies, multiple reinforcement and multiplier effects. A good example in this regard is the comprehensive disaster education program linking the school, family and community, developed by Kyoto University in cooperation with the Earthquake Disaster Mitigation Research Center and the National Research Institute for Earth Science and Disaster Prevention (Shaw et al., 2009b).

In any overview of the subject of education and natural disasters, what also needs to be acknowledged is the role that education has played in building our understanding of natural phenomena, and especially some of the giant leaps in understanding that have been made through the discoveries, theories and genius of key individuals. Whether this be the connection made between the movements of the moon and its effect on tides, the realisation that the earth is round, has a molten core, and the discovery of plate tectonics, the growing technological ability to forecast and communicate extreme weather events, or the discovery of the ozone layer and then a hole within it – all of this knowledge has transformed our understanding and the choices and responses we can make. It is beyond the scope of this book to take a historical angle by examining in detail the major contributions to knowledge of physicists, geologists, meteorologists, vulcanologists and other such specialists over the years, but the contribution of educational research in a contemporary perspective will be returned to briefly in what follows. Indeed, academic research is a fundamental component of education's contribution to natural disaster prevention, mitigation and response. Knowledge management is another important element of the equation. This itself has a number of key strands, including monitoring and evaluation, lessons-learning, knowledge-sharing and capacity-building.

Policy and Institutional Frameworks

The United Nations, through the United Nations International Strategy for Disaster Reduction (UNISDR), is today the apex agency that provides leadership and policy frameworks in the field of natural disasters. UNISDR is unmatched in its position of being able to maintain and raise the status and visibility of disaster-related activities and issues, promote related development and research causes in the context of a global platform, and function as a clearing house for information dissemination. United Nations involvement can be traced back to at least the 1960s – a decade during which several UN resolutions were passed in response to specific severe natural disasters that occurred during this period. Subsequent historical milestones have included the creation of the United Nations Disaster Relief Office in 1971 and the declaration of the period 1990–9 as the International Decade for Natural Disaster Reduction and the benefits and progress this brought, including the convening of a World Conference on Disaster Reduction, in 1994 in Yokohama, Japan (UNISDR, 2011c).

UNISDR was created in December 1999, as the successor to the secretariat of the International Decade for Natural Disaster Reduction, with the purpose of ensuring the implementation of the International Strategy for Disaster Reduction. The mandate of UNISDR expanded in 2001 to serve as the focal point in the United Nations system for the coordination of disaster reduction and to ensure synergies among the disaster-reduction activities of the United Nations system and regional organizations and activities in socio-economic and humanitarian fields. This was in response to a need for mainstreaming disaster risk-reduction within the development and other areas of work of the UN.

A Second World Conference on Disaster Reduction was held in Kobe, Hyogo, Japan, in January 2005. This conference adopted the present 'Hyogo Declaration' and the 'Hyogo Framework for Action 2005–2015: Building the Resilience of Nations and Communities to Disasters', adopted by 168 governments, which has come to be known as the Hyogo Framework. The outcome aimed for is 'the substantial reduction of disaster losses, in lives and in the social, economic and environmental assets of communities and countries' (UNISDR, 2005: 1). One of the five priorities for action expressly identified in the framework is concerned with education: 'Use knowledge, innovation and education to build a culture of safety and resilience at all levels' (ibid.). Specific areas identified include: knowledge management, such as information sharing and cooperation, and the further development and use of networks; the inclusion of disaster risk reduction content matter and approaches into school curricula; emphasis on informal education, especially public education and involving communities and local authorities, the raising of public awareness and the use of the media; and recognition of the importance of research and research capacity.

In November 2007, in support of the Hyogo Framework for Action, the UNISDR launched an information portal on disaster risk reduction called *PreventionWeb*. Its primary mandate is to facilitate the work of professionals involved in disaster risk-reduction and promote an understanding of the subject by non-specialists. *PreventionWeb*, now partnered by a host of development agencies, has quickly evolved into a major and unrivalled resource. To have accumulated so much knowledge and documentation under one easily accessible interface is a huge achievement. There is arguably no finer example of an internet database as a development resource. This is not to say that there are many more challenges and that *PreventionWeb* cannot be strengthened even further. Indeed, this chapter will put forward specific priority suggestions along these lines.

There are a number of other nodal agencies worthy of mention. These include: the Global Facility for Disaster Reduction and Recovery; the Global Network of Civil Society Organisations for Disaster Reduction; the Gender and Disaster Network; and the ProVention Consortium. All have their own web portals and it is encouraging to see that the majority partner each other and link to each other's websites – cohesion that is no doubt made easier by the fact that many common development agencies are involved in providing sponsorship. Whether activities, roles and responsibilities across these respective organisations could be further rationalised or disaggregated, to increase future cost-effectiveness, is perhaps a moot point.

Least well-covered under any of the umbrella portals is a way of capturing the very fragmented but nevertheless significant activity and interest that takes place within the private sector, especially with regard to capacity-building and the provision of response teams. While this is especially unfortunate, as a cohesive private sector database can be extremely helpful – especially for those seeking training and career opportunities – it is perhaps not surprising. Companies operating in a 'for profit' environment tend rightly to regard other businesses operating in the same field as commercial rivals, competing for the same clientele. They may feel a need to try to maintain a competitive advantage in order to stay in business or thrive: a mind-set that is not conducive to information-sharing, networking, or other forms of cooperation.

School Response

One of the most under-represented areas within the literature on education and natural disasters is the capture of knowledge on how schools have been able to respond to real-life disasters: the challenges they have been confronted with, the roles they have been required to play, how these have been faced, and the lessons that can be learnt from all of this. This is also a challenge for future research, especially with regard to any common themes that might emerge, even allowing for the fact that no disaster is the same in the impact it wreaks, and different levels of severity may well require different kinds of response. The chapters that follow in this volume make their own contribution to adding to this important area of knowledge through the case studies they describe.

It is also possible to paint here with a broad brush, in the context of a subject overview, the kinds of scenario that might typically unfold and how schools might respond. If schools are prepared, the emergency response may simply comprise implementing a 'school crisis plan'. Whether anticipated or not, among other things, emergency response might involve taking leading action and assisting: by working with emergency teams and local administrations in crisis management; triage activity determining who needs immediate assistance (medical and psychological); controlling media access and facilitating debriefings; communications between home and school; assessment of property damage and hazards; alerting other sites of possible impact; and planning transition academic and social activities (Oehler-Stinnett, et al., undated).

One of the challenges that schools will perhaps most often face, after the immediate emergency phase has ended, in disasters ranging from less severe to more severe, is the loss of the use of their premises through disaster damage. A key challenge is to provide a temporary solution so that schooling can be resumed as soon as possible. This is not only important from the perspective of providing educational continuity, but can be a key psychological factor in helping to contribute to a sense of a return to normality and helping to distract from disaster trauma. Solutions might include the use of temporary accommodation on site (tents, mobile classrooms, etc.) to the temporary dispersal of pupils to other schools that are undamaged, possibly by adopting a shift system of one kind or another, or using other facilities that can be adapted or borrowed for the purpose, from community halls to spare rooms in the premises of community leaders and businesses.

One further strategy that could be incorporated into an armoury of responses, and which has so far not been mainstreamed to the knowledge of this writer, is to reflect on the disaster mitigation and response potential of forming school clusters, where these do not already exist for other reasons. Educational literature is in any case strong on the benefits and value of school cluster arrangements (see, for example UNICEF, 2009: especially 12–13; and Dittmar et al., 2002). However, not typically included among identified benefits of cluster arrangements, such arrangements can also provide a ready-made support network in the event of a disaster and where all schools in the cluster are not affected equally by the disaster concerned. For example, if just one school has its buildings and facilities put out of action by, say, a flood or hurricane, other schools in the cluster can provide a support network in various ways, from lending equipment to temporarily accepting pupils from the stricken school until it is functional again. The support could also simply be in the form of physical and moral support in the clean-up operation – made possible by the collegiality that the cluster has engendered. Ideally, of course, schools in the cluster should evolve a cluster disaster-response strategy and policy ahead of an event, where there is a known significant risk of particular disasters occurring.

The potential of clustering is not limited to school-level arrangements only. As Morrissey (2007) has pointed out, in the context of the Commonwealth Caribbean: there is an opportunity for countries sharing common natural hazards to create clusters and networks, share information, and jointly develop and publish materials and resources. More will be said about this kind of institutional networking below. Additionally, further aspects of school response, such as providing post-emergency phase disaster counselling and implications for curriculum, will also be returned to below within discussion of 'the Role of Teachers' and 'Curriculum Content and Approaches'.

School Buildings and Safety

The desire to make a school building one of the strongest structures in a community is an aspect of disaster prevention and reduction that receives a large area of attention, both in subject literature and the practical and research responses that have been initiated and from which knowledge has been generated and lessons have been learnt. This desire is often informed by at least five key considerations. The first and foremost is the obvious desire to ensure that the school building will be able to protect the lives of children should a natural disaster occur unexpectedly during the normal school day. The second recognises that school buildings lend themselves to functioning as public shelters when an early warning of a natural disaster has been received. The third acknowledges the role that a school building can potentially play as an emergency shelter and/or operations centre after a natural disaster has occurred – anticipated or not. The fourth relates to the notion of resource preservation and cost-effectiveness. A school building is a major investment. Building a structure strong enough to resist natural hazards can avoid huge repair and rebuilding costs, more than offsetting any higher capital costs at the time of initial construction. The fifth is that:

> The vulnerability of school facilities must not be seen only in terms of the need to prevent catastrophic damage that may destroy the buildings. It is also necessary to prevent lesser damage that may affect the continuity of the services they provide. For example, if a school is unusable, the children will have to go to other schools, often in shifts, and their education suffers.
>
> (Caribbean Disaster Mitigation Project, 2001)

In the case of future new-build, or building renovation, considerations of this kind can inform the design and construction in at least two ways. The first is to do with structural strength or configuration (e.g. height of floors above ground level in the case of flooding) required to withstand the anticipated natural hazard. The second is to do with layout and the facilities that could be provided – such as ensuring that there is a large enough covered space to function normally as, say, a school assembly hall or gymnasium, but also serve as a community shelter in an emergency. The design, including placing and size, of school kitchens, water towers and sanitation facilities and access routes are further examples of layout considerations that may need to be taken into account. In large school structures, such as secondary schools, building areas may be zoned according to their potential emergency function. Indeed, where a particular natural hazard is particularly prevalent, such as earthquake or flooding risk, it is becoming far more commonplace for schools to be expressly designed and constructed to serve a dual function: routinely as a school, and as a community shelter in an emergency. A wealth of knowledge and experience has been generated and there is much good practice upon which to build. (See, for example: Arya, 1987; Darshan et al., 2009; Ghaidan, 2002; and ProVention Consortium, 2007).

It is also important to recognise that there are both structural and non-structural aspects of school safety. Structural safety issues include new-build design and materials issues of the kind identified above. They also include retrofitting challenges – making existing buildings safer. Training and public awareness are among non-structural aspects. This is especially significant where communities are involved in school management and maintenance. There are implications for those involved in school construction and maintenance, such as local masons and engineers. They need to be oriented and trained. Training materials and technical guidelines need to be developed. Documentation produced from experience in Nepal provides especially good illustrations of how considerations of this kind have been identified and addressed. (See, for example, NRCC, 2011). The Nepal experience also illustrates how making schools safe physically, especially with regard to retrofitting interventions, has three key dimensions that can be expressed in phases of time: conducting vulnerability assessments and drawing conclusions; conducting the physical works; and providing complementary training and awareness activities. In introducing or strengthening each of these dimensions there may also be education and training and other forms of capacity-building implications.

A further discrete and extremely important area of school safety relates to the drills and procedures put in place concerning how to behave in an emergency, should it occur. Again, this is an area in which considerable know-how has been built and excellent supporting resources developed. (See, for example, Ministry of Education, Sri Lanka, 2008). What should also not be overlooked is that model behaviours of this kind often do not just develop by themselves. Programmes of awareness raising, training, and resource dissemination, and networks of support and supervision, may also need to be put in place to trigger and sustain them. Furthermore, all these elements can themselves have associated capacity-building considerations: who trains the trainers and supervisors, who develops the training programmes and materials, and so on?

Education and Natural Disasters Curriculum Content and Approaches in the School Milieu

The advocacy of mainstreaming teaching and learning on natural disasters into the school curriculum is one of the most commonly recurring strategies in disaster risk reduction policy statements, publications and resource materials. It is worth reflecting a little further here on some of the different ways that natural disaster related content can be incorporated into the school milieu – especially as much of the literature does not provide this level of detail and perhaps leaving behind a false sense that there is only one way of doing this. In Table 1.1, a range of approaches is identified and described and some examples are provided of advantages and disadvantages associated with each kind of intervention.

Approach	Description	Advantages	Disadvantages
Curriculum integration	Discrete content on natural disasters is incorporated into the curriculum of existing subjects such as geography, science, maths, social studies and language. This can be through the inclusion of specific units and modules. It can be through a spectrum of other approaches that might, for instance, accord with Fogarty's (1991) ten models of curriculum integration: fragmented; connected; nested; sequenced; shared; webbed; threaded; integrated; immersed; and networked.	The content is genuinely mainstreamed, therefore its inclusion is likely to remain sustainable.	Many curricula are already overloaded. Adding more content only increases the strain.
Stand-alone courses	Specialized course content focused on natural disasters	Allows for more in-depth and systematic study.	More likely to be feasible only to introduce as a subject option/elective, rather than as a part of the core curriculum, limiting the number of individuals exposed and impacted.
Project work	Natural disasters become a theme for a one-off, intensive period of study. In the primary school, there is usually an opportunity to incorporate all the subjects of the curriculum in the project.	Projects are often stimulated by, and coincide with, something topical that has occurred, maximising the potential to build on and create interest, and for learners to appreciate the relevance of the content.	Inclusion of natural disaster-related project choices is far from guaranteed.
Incidental teaching opportunities	A natural disaster-related event, which may be local or international, has occurred and is used as a point of reference, e.g. as a contextual example, during the teaching process, if only briefly.	Arouses curiosity and makes learning content more real and meaningful.	Relies heavily on teacher creativity and initiative. Incidental opportunities are by their very nature unpredictable and sporadic. They cannot be relied upon to occur and may not materialise at a convenient time in the teaching process.

Extra-curricular activities	Can include out-of-school hours activities such as clubs, and school in the community initiatives (e.g. a tree planting campaign to address deforestation), the promotion of natural disaster-themed educational games, and the use of competitions (such as poster design competitions) to raise awareness and interest.	High potential impact when ideas are new and fresh and capture the imagination.	Impact often declines and interest wanes once the newness of the idea/ activity wears off or it is repeated. It can be difficult to keep thinking of something new and fresh to maintain interest. It can be difficult to sustain the effort involved.
Supplementary Materials	Students are exposed to reading books, general interest and reference books that have been developed to be based upon or include natural disaster-related content.	Offer great flexibility: from being chosen as leisure reading from a library, to serving as key resource material for personal research on an allocated or chosen subject, or in support of specific teaching themes.	Not all students are avid readers.
The Hidden Curriculum	Can include, for example: the choice of posters displayed on walls; and the attitudes and behaviours modelled by teachers towards safety and disaster preparedness. It can also include school policy on safety drills and procedures and the level of seriousness and interest with which these are followed.	Has strong potential to impact upon behaviours and attitudes, not simply cognitive learning.	Not everyone is comfortable with the notion of setting out to shape people's minds and behaviours through deliberate covert methods.

Table 1.1 Education and Natural Disasters in the School Milieu

For the successful adoption into schools of any of the approaches identified above, there are likely to be implications for teacher training. Consequently, there are knock-on effects, too, for teacher training content. For changes to the formal curriculum, policy approval is likely to be involved. It should also be remembered that the real curriculum 'is not what the planners plan but what teacher actually does in the classroom' (Cundy, 1977: 7). There is a strong tendency for many teachers to 'teach from the textbook' and/or 'teach to the test'. For maximum impact, especially at post-primary level, textbooks need to be modified to include natural disasters-related content and examples, and examination questions need to explore aspects of the same subject matter. Thus there are further implications here for the orientation of textbook writers and examiners. This may involve capacity-building/training and/or policy edict.

Teachers can also be trained and encouraged to develop their own materials and lesson plans, rather than relying on published materials. For teacher training programmes to be designed and implemented effectively, it may be necessary to enlist the assistance of specialist non-governmental organisations. Examples exist of successful approaches of both of these kinds. (See, for instance Reye, 2011: 16–17, with regard to initiatives in Cambodia, Lao, Myanmar, the Philippines and Thailand). However, to avoid duplication of effort on the part of teachers, there is a future challenge to continue to develop and disseminate web-based resources where teacher-generated materials can be archived and accessed. The 'Educational Materials' collection available on *PreventionWeb*, featuring nearly 1950 items at the time of publication, provides access to curricular, extra-curricular and public awareness materials, including children's books, textbooks, lesson plans, activities, games and online resources on disaster prevention and school safety for primary, secondary, vocational, community-based education and public awareness. The collection is open for contributions and is maintained almost entirely by the Education and Disaster Risk Reduction community.

The Roles of Teachers in Disaster Response

Within the literature, roles are often envisioned for teachers as part of disaster response, going well beyond their normal duties and functions. These relate both to the immediate impact of any emergency and the longer-term recovery period. In respect of the former, teachers may be required to perform logistical, coordination and other operational roles as part of, say, search and recovery. This is more likely to be the case particularly in less-developed rural areas where the teacher is typically held in high regard in a local community and looked up to for knowledge, guidance and leadership. There is a paradox here, as well as in other contexts, that teachers in remote areas may well have less capacity than their counterparts in urban settings, yet more is often demanded of them!

At the same emergency stage, teachers are also often identified as being potential first-aiders, especially if professional medical assistance is not readily or immediately available. However, teachers need to be given the wherewithal and confidence to perform such roles. This is likely to include training and capacity-building, the development and communication of pre-agreed operational procedures – including, for example, setting up networking arrangements with local hospitals and other emergency and support services – and the regular practising of appropriate drills.

With regard to longer-term recovery, a principal theme that emerges frequently from relevant literature concerns post-traumatic stress and other emotional disorders such as grief and depression. Pararas-Carayannis (undated) is among those who argue that teachers have 'a responsibility to address social, emotional and psychological problems that may result in the post-disaster phase, particularly among their students', but also in the wider community. However, like others, he also recognises that:

> teachers and educators cannot be responsible for the treatment of all the emotional and psychological problems of the community that may result from a disaster. However, they can be of great help to the children in their schools, if they can understand these problems.
>
> (Pararas-Carayannis, undated)

For teachers to play such a role, programmes of preparedness will need to be well organised prior to any disaster. Among other things, teachers will need to be trained and supported with networks in place. Gauthamadas is an example of an excellent resource providing practical know-how for building interventions of this kind. However, this source rightly cautions that teachers themselves are also emotionally vulnerable, just like any other human beings; moreover, 'because of their leadership roles, it may be difficult … to acknowledge that they, too, could benefit from psychosocial services' (Gauthamadas, 2005: 27).

Non-Formal and Informal Education, Including Public Education

Non-formal and informal educational approaches and interventions, especially through the work of non-governmental organisations in rural and impoverished urban areas, have a huge role to play in helping to prevent and reduce the prevalence and impact of natural disasters. Such an assertion is made, among other things, in cognisance that a strong correlation has been established at the outset between poverty, levels of education, and the impact and prevalence of natural disasters. Non-formal and informal educational initiatives can be an especially important means of access *for* and *to* those who have never attended school, dropped out of basic education or otherwise underachieved – giving them a second chance. Non-formal and informal education mechanisms are crucial for: transmitting appropriate educational and developmental messages; changing attitudes, knowledge and behaviours; helping to develop livelihood skills; and sensitising the disempowered to their, civil, legal and human rights. There are manifest ways in which all these angles can be given a natural hazard and natural disaster focus.

Public education is just one dimension of non-formal and informal education, but it is an especially important one. Therefore the opportunity will be taken here to use public education as an exemplar area to highlight some of the many possibilities that non-formal and informal education can offer. Table 1.2 therefore provides an illustrative spectrum of educational focus and content for public education, in the context of disaster risk-reduction, identified by the IFRC (2011).

The Role and Contribution of the Private Sector, Including Public/Private Partnerships

Countries such as the UK and the USA appear to have significant private sector interest and involvement in human capacity-building in relation to natural disasters. Typically, playing a role in this area appears to be seen as both a commercial opportunity as well as a way of doing good. As has been noted above, unfortunately, the former consideration does militate against information sharing and, from a development perspective, it discourages making oneself redundant by building the capacity of other institutions in the developing world to take over this kind of role. There is a manifest lack, but a need for, better databases, e.g. at *PreventionWeb*, to obtain a more comprehensive picture of what is going on: where capacity exists and where there are development challenges to build capacity. These databases can also help institutions to inter-connect, where there is a will to do so, and they can help match people and institutions who are looking for services, or seeking

Assessment and planning	Vulnerability and capacity assessment	• Hazard identification • Vulnerability and capacity assessment • Hazard, vulnerability and resource mapping
	Planning and advocacy	• Community-based disaster preparedness planning • Integrated community planning • Family disaster planning • Safe land-use planning • Business continuity planning • Educational continuity planning • Legislative advocacy • Insurance planning
	Early warning systems	• End-to-end early warning systems • Early warning message formulation, delivery and verification • Evacuation planning
Physical and environmental mitigation	Structural and non-structural safety	• Safe land-use practices • Disaster-resilient construction (homes, schools, health facilities) • Retrofitting existing construction • Building and maintaining shelters and safe havens • Fastening tall and heavy furnishings against earthquake shaking • Fastening equipment and arranging supplies to safeguard against shaking • Making sure doors open outwards • Raising supplies and assets above flood levels • Advocacy for building code development and enforcement
	Infrastructure safety, including water and sanitation	• Evacuation route construction • Solid waste management • Clearing flood channels • Landslide mitigation • Household water supply and treatment • Water conservation (including rainwater harvesting, groundwater recharge, run-off catchments and sand dams) • Watershed clean-ups • Eco-san recycling toilets • Energy conservation • Clean and renewable energy for heating, cooking and lighting (including solar, wind and water pumps)
	Food security and livelihood protection	• Wetland and coastal restoration • Forestation and reforestation • Restoration of biodiversity • Crop selection for drought adaptation • School and community gardens • Vocational training
	Health	• Hygiene and sanitation promotion • Environmental health surveillance • Awareness to prevent airborne and water-borne diseases • Insecticide-treated mosquito nets • Malaria prophylaxis and treatment • Oral rehydration education • Condom distribution
Preparedness, response and recovery	Preparedness skills, psychosocial support, community-based first aid	• Drills, tabletop exercises and simulations • Early warning compliance and evacuation • Organization of response • Light search and rescue • First aid skills • Mass casualty triage • Psychological first aid • Life skills and conflict resolution • Swimming lessons • Wireless communications
	Response provisioning	• Emergency water and food supplies and storage • First aid supplies (such as standardized first aid kit guidance) • Life jackets and flotation devices • Emergency communications equipment • Emergency shelter supplies

Based on: 'Table 2: Integrating public education for disaster reduction'. International Federation of Red Cross and Red Crescent Societies (IFRC), 2011. *Public Awareness and Public Education for Disaster Risk Reduction: A Guide*. IFRC: Geneva, 19–20. Used with permission.

Table 1.2 A Spectrum of Educational Focus and Content for Public Education, in the context of Disaster Risk-Reduction

to work with a service provider. Among PreventionWeb's themes is 'Public-private Partnerships'. A section of the Portal aims to provide an overview of private sector engagement developing partnerships with government by promoting who's doing what and where (www.preventionweb.net/english/themes/ppp/). Private sector engagement in disaster risk-reduction is ever increasing, including through an advisory group to the UNISDR and the Disaster Risk Reduction Private Sector Partnership (DRR-PSP). Joining this partnership may be of interest to DRR capacity-development specialists in the private sector (see: www.unisdr.org/partners/private-sector).

Private sector activity can either take the form of diversification from a core strand of activity not directly related to natural disasters, or comprise a dedicated institutional business/purpose that is directly related. It is helpful to provide a few illustrative examples. However, it should be cautioned that these may not necessarily be representative of the nature of private sector provision as a whole, simply because data are so lacking.

In the UK, The Royal National Lifeboat Institution (RNLI) is one of the country's most respected charities set up to save lives at sea, with a history that can be traced back to 1824. Its mainstream work involves the provision and manning of lifeboats and lifeguard services at strategic places around the UK's coastal waters. However, in 2000, the RNLI diversified its services by forming a flood rescue team to provide systematic emergency response both in the UK and abroad. First international deployment of the team took place in 2005, in Guyana. The RNLI's involvement in international recovery can however be traced back to 1970 and involvement in international flood-relief efforts in Bangladesh. Additionally, the RNLI offers training services in related areas of work. It has a dedicated training college with a commercial arm – the income from which helps to fund the RNLI's mainstream work. Among other things, the RNLI offers training programmes to staff from search and rescue organisations throughout the world and offers modules expressly related to flood response (RNLI, 2011).

'Rescue3' is an example of a UK-based commercial training and consultancy provider, also with a water-based focus. Its training programmes include various forms of rescue from water, flood operations for emergency planners, as well as courses with an awareness focus. Unlike the RNLI, Rescue3's current client base is entirely UK focused. Even so, Rescue3 still emphasises that it provides internationally recognised rescue training. It typically trains mountain rescue teams, members of the UK's emergency services: the police, fire and ambulance services (Rescue3, 2011). This is an important point to note: many people who receive training and acquire qualifications related to natural hazards and disasters in the private sector do this not to pursue careers dedicated to natural hazards and disasters but to be on stand-by for roles in the event of an emergency, as part of other mainstream careers, where these careers have some kind of natural overlap. Furthermore, the courses provided in the private sector are typically short, intensive practical courses of a few days or few weeks duration to enhance the specialist skills of people already in jobs in related areas of work. This is in contrast to the academic programmes more typically provided in public institutions such as universities, of the kind that will be discussed below. In many cases, these programmes – especially at undergraduate level – are followed as part of a pathway towards an aspiring career directly related to the programme of study.

It is almost certain that the private sector patterns described above are what other less-developed and more disaster-prone countries are trying to follow and emulate, even though information about such developments is harder to glean. It is noted, for example, that, in 2008, China set up its own 'National Earthquake Rescue Training Base' to 'mainly provide training sessions for three groups of people: the National Earthquake Rescue Team and the provincial rescue teams; emergency administrative staff at all levels; and social volunteers, particularly core volunteers'.

One basis for drawing attention to the importance and potential of public/ private partnerships is that 'disaster risk-reduction is everybody's business' (UNISDR, 2011a). An important role is also envisaged, by some, for private-public sector collaboration to enhance community disaster resilience. A recent workshop report has attempted to capture the current state of the art in this regard and make future recommendations (Committee on Private-Public Sector Collaboration to Enhance Community Disaster Resilience, 2010). It takes a United States focus, and is not confined to disasters of nature, but many of its findings and conclusions have a wider resonance. Among other things, it draws attention to key motivators, inhibitors, advantages and liabilities for private sector engagement, for instance: the role and importance of leadership, scalability, trust, challenges created by political jurisdictions and language barriers.

Global Hand (2010) provides a good example of some pointers to the 'why', 'what' and 'how' of private sector engagement. These range from the humanitarian imperative to enlightened self-interest. Despite the above, a strong sense emerges from a review of relevant literature that public/private partnership is a nascent area, especially in less developed and transitional regions (see, for example, Roeth, 2009), and even more so in respect of educational dimensions per se. Few success stories have been captured and this is a challenge for future research.

Further and Higher Education: with particular reference to an analysis of the range of academic programmes offered through *PreventionWeb*

Further and higher education plays a very important role in contributing to building human capacity to prevent, prepare for, manage and respond to natural disasters. It also plays a major role in the development of understanding of the subject, as a result of the research activity that takes place within these institutions.

In this section of the chapter, the opportunity is taken to conduct a selective statistical analysis and qualitative commentary in relation to academic programmes publicised on the *PreventionWeb* website in 2011. The intention is to gauge the kind and extent of coverage, reveal key patterns, and consider questions of balance and imbalance. The academic programmes listed are not exhaustive of the educational opportunities relating to natural disasters available globally, but they are by far the most definitive resource. The scope of the *PreventionWeb* Academic Programmes collection is that the courses must be provided by accredited higher education institutions and/or offer university credit. For all other training, sometimes offered or hosted by private companies, the courses would appear in the Training & Events Calendar under 'training'. It is a significant achievement and important contribution to knowledge that *PreventionWeb* is able to provide a database of this kind. At the same time, there is a challenge to make it even more comprehensive in future. For example, there are significant private sector providers (along the lines of examples identified above) whose programmes are not catalogued within the *PreventionWeb* database.

An initial important observation is just how many programmes are on offer across the world: a total of 192 publicised academic programmes, as of August 2011, in 31 different countries. What the statistics do not show is how this provision is changing over time, reflecting any variation in levels of interest and importance attached to the subject. Data of this kind will certainly be worth monitoring in the future. It is a fairly safe assumption, however, with increased awareness of global warming and other environmental issues, that natural disasters currently constitute a growing area of academic interest.

Programmes on offer are extremely diverse, when classified by programme content as indicated by title; yet the majority are broad-based. For example, of the 192 programmes on offer, eighty-five (44.3%) contain the phrases 'disaster/ emergency/risk management'. Some courses focus on specific risk such as flood risk, or specific technical aspects of risk such as infrastructure. There are also seemingly unique programmes on offer. The University of Calgary in Canada, for instance, is distinctive in offering a masters programme in applied snow and avalanche research.

Figure 1.1 (A) provides a summary of how the 192 programmes are disaggregated by programme type. *PreventionWeb* uses a classification system of five programme types: University Programme; Online Courses; Continuing Education; Distance Learning; Blended Programme. Some explanation of the categories will be helpful. All the listed programmes are offered in a university or equivalent academic environment. The term 'university programme' indicates a programme followed in a university or equivalent by the conventional means, that is to say, as a full-time student studying on campus. 'Online courses', 'continuing education', and 'distance learning' refer to other means of studying within the university or equivalent environment using flexible modalities conventionally associated with these terminologies. A 'blended programme' is a programme offered through a range of levels: e.g. certificate/diploma, bachelor and masters levels. This provides students with opportunities to enter and leave programmes at different academic intervals according to interests, needs and educational backgrounds. As Figure 1.1 (A) shows, a broad range of coverage is provided across the five levels, but with conventional university programmes representing by far the dominant modality. What the statistics do not show, however, is how well-matched or otherwise is what is offered with what is demanded. For example, do far more students seek to study by continuing education mode than there are places available, or do continuing education courses not get filled to capacity? It is a challenge to *PreventionWeb* and other organisations to try to gather and publicise statistics of this kind. It can lead to important findings that will help providing institutions in their future planning and provide would-be students with a better idea of their chances of making a successful application.

Another important observation to make is that all 192 programmes are offered by universities or equivalent institutions of substantial national and

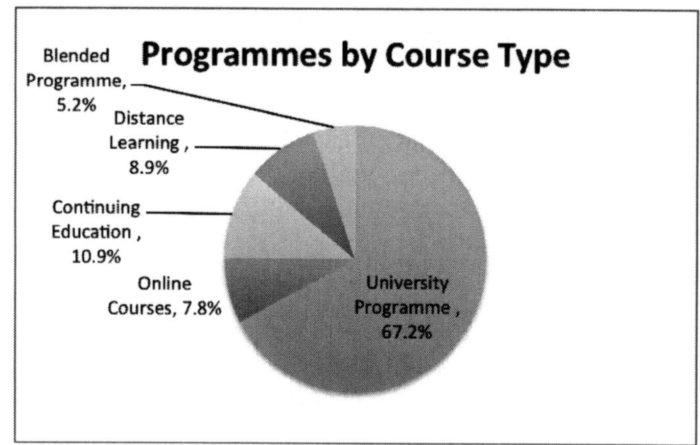

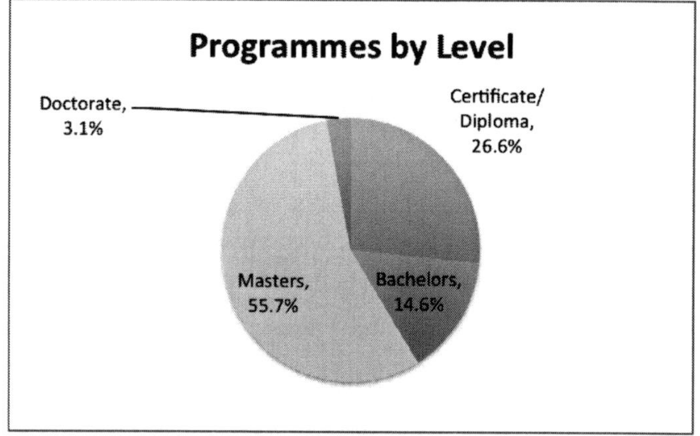

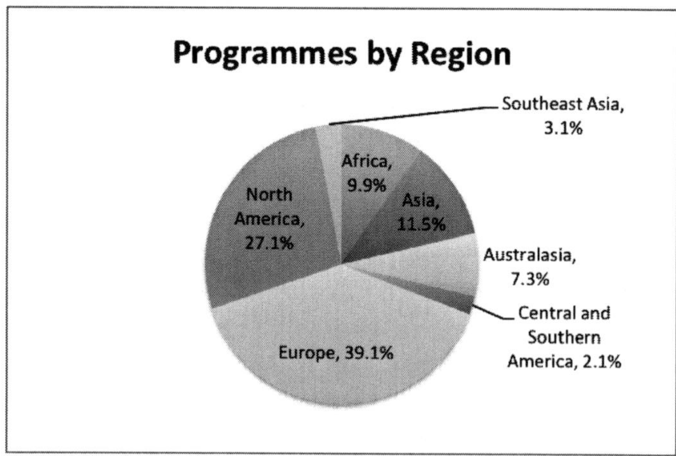

Figure 1.1 A Statistical Analysis of Academic Programmes Related to Natural Disasters, Publicised by Prevention Web

international repute. Furthermore, all programmes lead to conventional academic qualifications. This augurs well for quality assurance and recognition of qualifications, including national and international mobility.

Figure 1.1 (B) shows how the data for the 192 different programmes can be disaggregated by level of study. *PreventionWeb* uses four categorisation levels: certificate/diploma; bachelors; masters; and doctorate. Figure 1.1 (B) shows that coverage across all four levels is broad, but that masters level study, comprising 55.7% of all programmes offered, is by far the more dominant programme. Again, what the statistics are unable to reveal, is the extent of any match or mismatch of supply and demand. Information of this kind, if it can be made available, will again greatly assist forward institutional and policy planning and help applicants in making their choices.

An attempt has also been made here to shed light in relation to the language in which programmes are transacted. For this purpose, the assumption has been made that where a course or programme has been listed in a language other than English, the course is offered in that language. This may not necessarily be a correct assumption in all cases, so any conclusions in this regard should be seen as tentative. However, what such an analysis shows is that of the 192 programmes on offer, 180 (93.8%) appear to be offered in English and just 12 (6.3% of the total) in languages other than English (e.g. French and Spanish). It seems highly plausible, therefore, that language of instruction could be a significant barrier to entry for some potential candidates. This is an area that is important enough to demand further research and possible policy remediation if access issues are indeed confirmed.

Figure 1.1 (C) and Table 1.3 are presented to illuminate patterns of provision by country and region. While confirming some broadness of coverage they also appear to expose some important imbalances that could pose future policy challenges.

Taking, Figure 1.1 (C) first: programme coverage has been disaggregated by the author of this chapter across seven geographical regions: Africa; Asia; Australasia; Central and Southern America; Europe; North America; and Southeast Asia. It has already been established at the outset that natural disasters tend to occur more frequently and with greater severity and consequences in less developed regions of the world. It would therefore perhaps seem reasonable to expect programme provision relating to natural disasters to be more prevalent and more relevant in less-developed regions. As far as prevalence is concerned, however, quite the opposite pattern emerges

Region	Number of Programmes by Region	Country	Number of Programmes by Country
Africa	19	Kenya	11
		South Africa	7
		Egypt	1
Asia	22	Bangladesh	5
		India	5
		Thailand	5
		Japan	3
		Pakistan	2
		Nepal	1
		Sri Lanka	1
Australasia	14	Australia	8
		New Zealand	6
Central and South America	4	Chile	2
		Nicaragua	1
		Peru	1
Europe	75	United Kingdom	39
		France	10
		Netherlands	10
		Switzerland	6
		Denmark	4
		Italy	2
		Germany	1
		Poland	1
		Spain	1
		Sweden	1
North America	52	Canada	11
		United States of America	41
Southeast Asia	6	Indonesia	2
		Malaysia	2
		Hong Kong	1
		Philippines	1

Table 1.3 Number of Academic Programmes related to Natural Disasters, by Country and Region, Publicised by Prevention Web in 2011

from the statistics. Europe and North America for example, account for the location of 66.2% of all programmes publicised on the *PreventionWeb* database. Conversely, programmes offered in Africa, by way of developing and vulnerable region example, account for just 9.1% of total programmes.

Focusing more precisely on countries rather than regions, just six countries – the United States of America; the United Kingdom; Canada; Kenya; France; and the Netherlands – account for 63.5% of all programmes publicised on the *PreventionWeb* database. Only Kenya is a developing country. The United Kingdom, one of the least vulnerable nations on the planet to natural disasters, offers 20.3% of all programmes on the database, second only to the United States (21.3%). As is well known, the United States and the United Kingdom are among the biggest recipients and beneficiaries of international student mobility and it seems highly likely (though not statistically proven in the current analysis) that programmes related to natural disasters offered by developed countries attract large numbers of international students from less-developed countries. A considerable part of the explanation is likely to be a financial imperative. International student mobility is big business. This is not to deny that more-developed nations may genuinely have world-leading expertise to offer. It also is only fair to recognise that individuals still benefit, since many of them will then return to their home countries and put their knowledge and expertise to important use in positions of seniority and leadership.

Nevertheless, what may be occurring are core-periphery relationships, where the advantaged core tends to benefit disproportionately from the disadvantaged peripheries. Grounds for suspecting this kind of phenomenon are also increased by focusing on Africa. As Table 1.3 shows, with the exception of just one programme offered in Egypt, two important 'hubs' in the continent seem to dominate completely the academic provision available: Kenya and South Africa. This is not necessarily an invidious finding. It might be reasonable and cost-effective to justify the promotion of regional centres of excellence when resources are limited and where it may not be feasible to promote specialist provision in every nation state. Kenya is home to the International Center for Emergency Preparedness Training (INTER-CEPT). South Africa hosts the African Centre for Disaster Studies (ACDS). However, the appropriateness or otherwise of the patterns discussed here is crucially important and deserves future policy reflection.

What is felt to be easily the greatest overriding implication of the discussion so far presented is to do with recognition that capacity-building can be considered as having two important forms: the capacity-building of individuals and the capacity-building of institutions. On the basis of the broad range of relevant programmes on offer, in institutions of great repute, there are strong grounds for confidence that these programmes collectively make a huge contribution to developing individual capacity. But what of institutional capacity-building? The discussion above points to how current institutional capacity, expertise and know-how, as reflected in academic programmes on offer in the *PreventionWeb* database, resides disproportionately in developed country institutions. A key future policy challenge is how the transfer of institutional capacity from more-developed to less-developed academic institutions can be encouraged and promoted as far as natural disasters expertise and know-how is concerned. One of the most proven ways to promote institutional capacity-building in higher education is through programmes such as Erasmus Mundus, as evidenced by Smawfield and Leowinata (2010). Erasmus Mundus promotes academic mobility of students and staff. Crucially, it also promotes Joint and Double degree arrangements that appear to benefit all the participating institutions as well as the participating students and academics themselves.

It is felt strongly by this writer that there is an enormous policy opportunity to promote more actively joint and double degrees and exchange programmes between institutions with an active interest in the field of natural disasters. Currently, among the 192 programmes on offer, just one (an Erasmus Mundus MSc in flood risk management, offered by the UNESCO–IHE Institute for Water Education in the Netherlands) is manifestly a programme with exchange, double or joint degree opportunities – and hence with overt mechanisms for institutional knowledge transfer and capacity-building.

A feature of the Erasmus Mundus model is that it requires universities to establish Consortia i.e. groups of universities that function collaboratively. There is also evidence (Smawfield and Leowinata, 2010) that Consortium arrangements can themselves help to build capacity among Consortium members through the academic and administrative interchange that takes place. Furthermore, Erasmus Mundus tendering specifications can be, and sometimes are, structured in ways that encourage or require universities in advanced regions to partner with universities in less-developed regions. Among other things, in the context of the subject under discussion, this can help institutions that do not have an academic track record relating to natural disaster expertise, programmes and research, to build their capacity through mentoring arrangements with other institutions within a region: for example, by setting up joint programmes. The term 'region' here can refer both to regions involving several nations and regions within nations. There is much that can be learnt from this approach. It can be pursued either within the Erasmus Mundus model, through similar mechanisms, or through new creative thinking and initiatives that will inspire similar forms of institutional capacity-building collaboration.

The Role of Research

It is probably safe to say that where research plays roles in other fields, the potential of research to contribute to understanding of the causes of natural disasters, prevention, mitigation, response and recovery, and the modalities through which it can do this, are no less broad. For example, research has led to technological discoveries, such as the ability to launch and use satellites, to provide the tools to monitor natural phenomena and provide early warnings. It has contributed to the development of drought- and disease-resistant plants and crops that can help to address desertification. It has yielded knowledge on the kinds of structures and building methods that produce the most seismically resistant school buildings. Research has led to a greater understanding of cause and effect relationships. It plays a crucial role in forming needs assessment. Perhaps more mundanely, but no less importantly, research in the form of monitoring and evaluation plays an important role in helping to gauge the extent to which plans are being kept on track and whether or not there are better ways of doing things.

As Cavallo and Noy point out, much research in the social sciences, and even more in the natural sciences, has been devoted to increasing our ability to predict disasters and prepare for them. There are gaps in understanding and the literature in other important areas. Cavallo and Noy themselves draw attention to how 'economic research on natural disasters and their consequences is fairly limited' (Cavallo and Noy, 2010: 6). Tighe (undated, 2) argues that 'there is room for research to answer the question, *what are the actual critical and systemic issues that are keeping people here vulnerable*?' [emphasis original]. An important role for research includes risk and vulnerability mapping. A major contribution in this area includes the work of Dilley, et al. (2005) that has led to the mapping of 'Natural Disaster Hotspots: A Global Risk Analysis'. Nevertheless, as the researchers themselves acknowledge, work of this kind needs to be even more detailed and specific to have greater utility.

Conclusions

This chapter has shown how natural disasters have human, economic and environmental manifestations and implications. It has highlighted how some areas of the world and some sections of society are at far greater risk than others and how the consequences of disasters are far more severe. It has also provided insights into how education can and does play a vital role in prevention, mitigation, response and recovery: through formal education, non-formal education and informal education, and through some less conventional teacher-learner modalities learner, such as community-to-community learning, appreciation of the contribution of indigenous knowledge, and child-to-child and child-to-parent interaction.

By way of examples, this chapter has drawn attention to the existence of a very significant body of knowledge, practical documentary resources, institutional resources and networks, all supported by strong policy statements and frameworks. Collectively, this creates a very strong platform from which education is able to make such a significant contribution. Nevertheless, despite these achievements, of which the natural disaster-related professional community should rightly be proud, there are always challenges and opportunities to strengthen practice and capacity even further. Among practical ideas that have been put forward in this selective overview are: (i) the attention that has been drawn to the role that school clustering arrangements might play in strengthening response capacity and options; and (ii) a particularly important challenge to strengthen further academic networks, especially with a view to building institutional capacity. This second point is informed by observed imbalances, including core-periphery relationships, across developed, transitional and developing nations and regions. What is advocated is increased emphasis on international academic interchange focused on institutional capacity-building. This can be achieved through programmes such as Erasmus Mundus, in view of their conduciveness to the promotion of joint and double degree programmes, academic interchange (of staff as well as students) and collaborative research activity.

Acknowledgement

It is wished to express appreciation to Sarah Wade-Apicella, Managing Editor, PreventionWeb.net, UNISDR, who reviewed a draft of this chapter and provided extremely helpful constructive comments and criticism.

Questions for Further Consideration

1. The following are some of the themes explored in the broader series on 'Education as a Humanitarian Response': education systems and their functions; education as

> a global concern; education in emergencies; education and conflict; education, aid
> and aid agencies. (A) To what extent and in what ways (currently and potentially)
> are there commonalities and synergies with the theme explored here: education and
> natural disasters? (B) To what extent and in what ways does education and natural
> disasters constitute a unique area of humanitarian response?
> 2. Assuming the formulation of a future UN policy framework relating to natural
>   disasters, what should be its priority themes for education, to be built on what has
>   been achieved so far, and to address any gaps?

Suggestions for Further Reading

This 'Subject Overview' chapter has drawn on extensive references. All items within it are good candidates for further reading. Nevertheless, two web portals stand out as nodal points for further information access:

www.preventionweb.net This portal is updated daily. Its material is structured around: the Hyogo Framework; regions and countries; themes and issues; types of hazard; and professional resources. Among other things, its professional resources section provides information on: networks and communities; training and events; academic programmes; educational materials; jobs; terminology; documents and publications; and news and announcements.

www.unisdr.org The home page of the United Nations International Strategy for Disaster Risk Reduction. Resources and information are structured around: 'who we are'; 'what we do': 'where we work'; and 'who we work with'. The site is important for keeping abreast of policy developments and initiatives, upcoming disaster risk reduction events and news.

To help answer Question One, posed above: Brock, C. (2011). *Education as a Global Concern*. London: Continuum, provides an introduction to a number of issues covered in the 'Education as a Humanitarian Response' Series and some of their interrelationships.

References

All India Disaster Mitigation Institute (AIDMI) (2011). *Community-to-community learning*, 73, January. New Delhi: AIDMI. Available at: preventionweb.net/go/18624 [Accessed 8 September 2011].

Arya, A. S. (1987). *Protection of Educational Buildings Against Earthquakes: A Manual for Designers and Builders*. Bangkok: UNESCO. Available at: www.unesco.org/education/pdf/6_51.pdf#search=%22%22earthquake%20resistant%20schools%22%22 [Accessed 12 September 2011].

Boehn, D. L. (1996). Geographical education in Germany on natural disasters. In: J. Lidstone, *International Perspectives on Teaching about Hazards and Disasters*. Philadelphia: Clevedon, 33–8.

Cardona, O. D. (2007). Curriculum adaptation and disaster prevention in Columbia. In: J. P. Stoltman, J. Lidstone, and L. M Dechano, eds. *International Perspectives on Natural Disasters: Occurrence, Mitigation, and Consequences*. Dordrecht: Springer, 397–408.

Caribbean Disaster Mitigation Project (2001). *School/Shelter Hazard Vulnerability Reduction Resource Page*. Online. Available at: www.oas.org/CDMP/schools/schlrcsc.htm [Accessed 12 September 2011].

Cavallo, E. and Noy, I. (2010). *The Economics of Natural Disasters: A Survey*. IDB working paper series, 124. Washington, D.C.: Inter-American Development Bank. Available at: www.iadb.org/res/publications/pubfiles/pubIDB-WP-124.pdf [Accessed: 18 September 2011].

Child-to-Child Trust (2011). *Child-to Child Trust: Children Changing Their Lives*. Online. Available at: www.child-to-child.org [Accessed 23 September 2011].

Committee on Private-Public Sector Collaboration to Enhance Community Disaster Resilience; Geographical Science Committee; and National Research Council (2010). *Private-Public Sector Collaboration to Enhance Community Disaster Resilience: A Workshop Report*. Washington, D.C: National Academies Press. Available at: www.nap.edu/catalog.php?record_id=12864 [Accessed 22 September 2011].

Cundy, H. M. (1977). *Training the Teacher as the Agent of Reform: A Case Study of the Caribbean Mathematics Project, Experiments and Innovations in Education*. Geneva: UNESCO/IERS.

Darshan, S. H., Pribadi, K. S., Kusumastuti, D. and Limor, E. (2009). *Handbook of Typical School Design*. Bandung: Center for Disaster Mitigation, Institute of Technology Bandung/Save the Children International. Available at: preventionweb.net/go/17192 [Accessed 12 September 2011].

Dilley, M., Chen, R. S., Deichmann, U., Lerner-Lam, A. L. and Arnold, M. with Agwe, J., Buys, P., Kjekstad. O., Lyon, B. and Yetman, G. (2005). *Natural Disaster Hotspots: A Global Risk Analysis: Synthesis Report*. Washington, DC: The World Bank.

Dittmar, F., Mendelsohn, J. and Ward, V. (2002). *The School Cluster System in Namibia: Framework for Quality Education*. Windhoek: Ministry of Basic Education, Sport and Culture and the Deutsche Gesellschaft für Technische Zusammenarbeit (GTZ). Available at: www.raison.com.na/school_cluster.pdf [Accessed: 18 September 2011].

Fogarty, R., ed. (1993). *Integrating the Curricula: A Collection*. Palatine: IRI/Skylight Publishing.

Gauthamadas, U. (2005). *Disaster Psychosocial Response Handbook for Community Counselor Trainers*. Chennai: Academy for Disaster Management Education Planning & Training (ADEPT). Available at: www1.reliefweb.int/rw/lib.nsf/db900sid/SODA-6GP7S8/$file/handbook_for_community_counselor_trainers.pdf?openelement [Accessed 12 September 2011].

Ghaidan, U. (2002). *Earthquake Resistant Masonry Buildings: Basic Guidelines for Designing Schools in Iran*. Paris: UNESCO. Available at: portal.unesco.org/education/en/file_download.php/781 02a04b4136a3210aaccf675ba2748earthquake_iran.pdf#search=%22%22earthquake%20%20 resistant%22%20schools%22 [Accessed 12 September 2011].

Gitter, S. R. and Barham, B. L. (1999). Credit, natural disasters, coffee, and educational attainment in rural Honduras. *World Development* [online] Available at: new.aae.wisc.edu/research/development/publications/gitter-barham-w%20dev%2007.pdf [Accessed 15 June 2011].

Global Hand (2010). *Disaster Risk Reduction and the Private Sector: The Why, What, How of Engagement.* Hong Kong: Global Hand. Available at: www.globalhand.org/system/assets/49d316f3 8830f8e8f0c893b1c9ee8369918d2b88/original/Disaster_Risk_Reduction_and_the_private_sector.pdf [Accessed 22 September 2011].

International Federation of Red Cross and Red Crescent Societies (IFRC) (2010). *Children in Disasters – Games and Guidelines to Engage Youth in Risk Reduction.* Bangkok: IFRC. Available at: preventionweb.net/go/16726 [Accessed 8 September 2011].

—(2011). *Public Awareness and Public Education for Disaster Risk Reduction: A Guide.* Geneva: IFRC. Available at: www.preventionweb.net/files/20158_302200publicawarenessddrguideenfina.pdf [Accessed 17 August 2011].

Ministry of Education (Sri Lanka) (2008). *Towards a Disaster Safe School: National Guidelines for School Disaster Safety.* Colombo: Ministry of Education/GTZ. Available at: www.preventionweb.net/files/9252_srinatguilines.pdf [Accessed 12 September 2011].

Morrissey, M. (2007). Curriculum innovation for natural disaster reduction: lessons from the Commonwealth Caribbean. In: J. P. Stoltman, J. Lidstone, and L. M Dechano, eds. *International Perspectives on Natural Disasters: Occurrence, Mitigation, and Consequences.* Dordrecht: Springer, 385–96.

Nepal Risk Reduction Consortium (NRCC) (2011). *Disaster Risk Reduction in Nepal Flagship Programmes.* Kathmandu: NRCC. Available at: reliefweb.int/sites/reliefweb.int/files/resources/Full_Report_256.pdf [Accessed 17 August 2011].

Oehler-Stinnett, J., Cruise, C. and Marcantel (undated). *Natural Disasters: School Psychology's Role.* PowerPoint Presentation. Available at: www.nasponline.org/prepare/cpipresentations/natural%20disasters.ppt [Accessed 22 September 2011].

Pararas-Carayannis, G. (undated) *Natural Disasters.* Online. Available at: www.drgeorgepc.com/NaturalDisasters.html [Accessed 15 June 2011].

ProVention Consortium (2007). *Tools for Mainstreaming Disaster Risk Reduction: Construction Design, Building Standards and Site Selection.* Geneva IFRC/ProVention Consortium. Available at: www.proventionconsortium.org/themes/default/pdfs/tools_for_mainstreaming_GN12.pdf [Accessed 12 September 2011].

Rescue3. (2011). *Welcome to Rescue 3 (UK).* Online. Available at: www.rescue3.co.uk/index.htm [Accessed 22 September 2011].

Reye, M. L., ed. (2011). *Disaster Resilience Starts with the Young: Mainstreaming Disaster Risk Reduction in the School Curriculum.* Jakarta: ASEAN.

Roeth, H. (2009). *Consultancy Project on the Development of a Public Private Partnership Framework and Action Plan for Disaster Risk Reduction (DRR) in East Asia: Final Report.* Hong Kong: Corporate Social Responsibility Asia. Available at: www.preventionweb.net/files/10840_UNISDR.pdf [Accessed 22 September 2011].

Royal National Lifeboat Institution (RNLI) (2011). *What We Do*. Online. Available at: www.rnli.org. uk/what_we_do [Accessed 22 September 2011].

Samant, L. D., L. Tobin, T. and Tucker, B. (2008). *Preparing Your Community for Tsunamis: A Guidebook for Local Advocates*. Palo Alto: GeoHazards International. Available at: www.geohaz. org/news/images/publications/PreparingYourCommunityforTsunamisVersion2-1.pdf [Accessed 26 June 2011].

Shaw, R. and Kobayashi, M. (2004). The role of schools in creating an earthquake-safer environment. In: Organisation for Economic Co-operation and Development (OECD) *Educational Facilities and Risk Management: Natural Disasters*. Paris: OECD, 41–8. Available at: www.oecdbookshop. org/oecd/display.asp?K=5LMQCR2JH4WJ&DS=Educational-Facilities-and-Risk-Management [Accessed 10 September 2011].

Shaw R., Sharma A. and Takeuchi Y. (2009). *Indigenous Knowledge and Disaster Risk Reduction: From Practice to Policy*. New York: NOVA Publications.

Shaw, R., Takeuchi, Y., Shiwaku, K., Fernandez, G., Gwee, Q. R. and Yang, B. (2009). *1-2-3 of Disaster Education*. Japan: Kyoto University. Available at: preventionweb.net/go/12088 [Accessed 10 September 2011].

Sims, J. (2007). Natural disasters and the role of women. In: J. P. Stoltman, J. Lidstone, and L. M Dechano, eds. *International Perspectives on Natural Disasters: Occurrence, Mitigation, and Consequences*. Dordrecht: Springer, 429–42.

Smawfield, D. and Leowinata, S. (2010), *External Evaluation of the Erasmus Mundus External Cooperation Window For India: Final Summary Report* New Delhi: European Union Delegation to India.

Tighe, K. (undated). *The Role of Research in Disaster Risk Reduction: Advanced Centre for Enabling Disaster Risk Reduction Research Brief 1*. Madurai: DHAN Foundation.

Toya, H. and Skidmore, M. (2007). Economic development and the impacts of natural disasters. *Economics Letters*, 94, 1, 20–5. Available at: sup.kathimerini.gr/xtra/media/files/fin/nat_skidmore. pdf [Accessed 15 June 2011].

United Nations Children's Fund (UNICEF) (2009). *Child-Friendly Schools Manual*. New York: UNICEF. Available at: www.unicef.org/publications/files/Child_Friendly_Schools_Manual_EN_040809.pdf [Accessed 18 September 2011].

United Nations Development Programme (UNDP) (2010). *UNDP Brief 7 – Gender and Disasters*. New York: Bureau for Crisis Prevention and Recovery/ UNDP. Available at: www.undp.org/cpr/documents/ disaster/7Disaster%20Risk%20Reduction%20-%20Gender.pdf [Accessed 17 September 2011].

United Nations Educational, Scientific and Cultural Organisation (UNESCO) (2007), *Natural Disaster Preparedness and Education for Sustainable Development*. Bangkok: UNESCO. Available at: www2. unescobkk.org/elib/publications/103/disaster.pdf [Accessed 24 June 2011].

United Nations International Strategy for Disaster Reduction (UNISDR) (2005). *Summary of the Hyogo Framework for Action 2005–2015: Building the Resilience of Nations and Communities to Disasters (Hyogo Framework)* Geneva: UNISDR. Available at: www.preventionweb.net/english/ professional/publications/v.php?id=8720 [Accessed 10 September 2011].

—(2011a). *Business Partnerships: Disaster Risk Reduction is Everybody's Business*. Geneva: UNISDR. Available at: www.preventionweb.net/files/18934_businessflyer.pdf [Accessed 22 September 2011].

—(2011b). *Disaster Risk Reduction*. Online. Available at: www.unisdr.org [Accessed 22 September 2011].

—(2011c). *History*. Online. Available at: www.unisdr.org/who-we-are/history [Accessed 22 September 2011].

World Health Organisation (WHO) (2008). *Integrating Emergency Preparedness and Response into Undergraduate Nursing Curricula*. Geneva: WHO. Available at: whqlibdoc.who.int/hq/2008/WHO_HAC_BRO_08.7_eng.pdf [Accessed 22 September 2011].

2

Bushfires in Australia: Learning to Live with Fire

Robin Burns

Chapter Outline

Introduction

Bushfires are a recurrent natural disaster throughout Australia. In this chapter, approaches to informing and educating the public to prevent, prepare for, respond to and recover from fires are reviewed. The occurrence of fires and the key agencies involved are outlined, followed by a review of major government inquiries into recent significant bushfire events. Three major areas of education concerning bushfires are then presented: adult community education, school education and the education of professionals. Throughout, issues of what sort of education, especially given population diversity, the question of risk perception and its role in establishing educational approaches and, where available, evaluations of programmes are presented. The focus is on the contexts for bushfire education and issues, rather than specific educational content.

Background: A Bushfire-prone Country

Australia is an ancient continent stretching 3860km from north to south, and nearly 4000km from east to west. There is evidence that 'bushfire' has been a risk since the continent began to become drier millions of years ago (CSIRO, 2008), a factor known and used by Aboriginal communities to align their seasonal patterns of hunting and gathering, assembling and dispersing. [The term 'bushfire' rather than 'wildfire' is adopted following the Report of the Royal Commission into the 2009 Victorian fires, and covers those fires that sweep through the countryside.] While summer is a season of heavy rains, cyclones and flooding in the tropical north, the southern half of the continent frequently dries out and is at its most bushfire prone. In the last decade there have been nearly 50 major fires in the southern states. The most destructive in terms of life lost was the February 2009 'Black Saturday' fires in the state of Victoria, when 173 people died, and there was extensive loss of property, wildlife and livestock, and habitat destruction. But every year bushfires occur across the continent (CFA, n.d.).

For most of southern Australia, if spring has been wet and lush there is a fast build-up of potentially flammable material that can dry out very quickly in a few hot weeks. During a dry spring, leaf litter and dead grasses accumulate, and trees and bushes weaken. The 2003 fires in the national capital, which caused four deaths and destroyed 188 homes, demonstrated that with the right wind and temperature conditions, a fire can roar out of control quickly and catastrophically, spreading from a nearby forest to devastate whole suburbs. With temperatures above 40°C and winds of 150kph and more, bushfire is a terrifying, deadly event.

Fires can be caused naturally or by human action or neglect. A dropped match in the right conditions can cause fires that burn for days, while branches falling on overhead powerlines may have disastrous consequences. Lightning strikes trigger around 25% of all bushfires, but even branches can ignite by rubbing together on a very hot, dry day, and once a fire has started, demons are released. Flying embers alighting on dry grass or littered house gutters burst into flame, and the oil in burning eucalypt trees explodes, spreading sparks, flaming bark and leaves. Such was the heat in the 2009 Victorian fires that trees were burnt down into their roots. Smoke during a fire, together with ash and other fire debris, can cause serious public health issues, especially if water sources become polluted. Rain after fire causes soil erosion, sometimes further damaging water catchments, and retarding regeneration of bushland despite the fact that some native plants only sprout after fire.

Over the past decade there have been major fires almost every summer, with the earliest fire in 2006 in spring (September). In that summer, the longest recorded fire burned for 69 days in remote mountainous country; three years later the greatest loss of life occurred (173). The greatest loss of property, however, was caused by the 1983 Ash Wednesday fires that spread across both Victoria and South Australia (CFA, op. cit.). With global warming evident in the rising average summer temperatures in southern Australia, and with the el Niño/la Niña cycles of drought and flood, there have been suggestions following the 2009 Victorian fires that some areas of the state are so fire-prone that residents should be relocated. Recent reports are quick to point out, however, that fire has always been an intimate part of the environment so the key to avoiding disastrous bushfires is learning to live with fire.

The Victorian Scenario

Since the subject of this chapter is bushfires and education, and since school education and emergency services in Australia are state responsibilities, the state of Victoria has been selected for this case study, with material from other states where relevant. Victoria, the smallest mainland state, is considered one of the most bushfire-prone places on earth. The record of fires involving huge areas and loss of at least ten lives goes back to 1851, when approximately one-quarter of the state burned.

The first line of defence against fires is the Country Fire Authority (CFA) and its urban relative, the Metropolitan Fire Brigade (MFB), together with the State Emergency Service (SES). Police are also involved, especially at the height of a fire outbreak, to manage the movement of people, to investigate arson or looting, and to assess and investigate casualties. Involved too is the Department of Sustainability and Environment (DSE), to assess risk and attempt vegetation clearance prior to summer, and during a fire for its knowledge of vegetation and landscape. Up-to-the-minute information on wind direction and temperature is provided by the Bureau of Meteorology (BoM). The health impacts of bushfires, the destruction or disruption of services and the displacement of people involve the Department of Human Services (DHS).

Thus the preparation for, management of and recovery from bushfires is complex, involving many organisations, so that a major factor at every stage of concern with bushfires is coordination and cooperation. The Royal Commission into the most recent Victorian fires (Parliament of Victoria, 2010; referred to throughout as the Royal Commission Report) drew urgent attention to this issue; it is repeatedly raised in community consultations and discussion with emergency organisations. In addition to the foregoing agencies, local government councils in fire-prone and affected areas have a role both before and after fires, providing information and facilities. Welfare organisations mobilise during and after a crisis, most notably the Australian Red Cross and the Salvation Army, but including many smaller community associations from churches to social groups. During the 2009 fires, the Zoo had to evacuate some animals from its Healesville property, where fire raged, and organisations both state and voluntary, concerned with National and State Parks and recreational facilities and the environment, all mobilise around major fire events. The state station of the national broadcaster, the Australian Broadcasting Commission (ABC), is the official site for radio warnings during a fire emergency. Other media hover, ever ready for a tragedy, a heroic tale or an anniversary. A notable absence from this list is educational institutions.

Government and people alike know the summer danger. However, the question arises after each fire season: what more could we have done to avert this? The reports after each major fire reveal great concern, analysis of causes and possible preventative strategies. Released soon after a major fire, they emphasise the recovery process for affected communities, though for those who have lost family, friends, property and livelihoods the reports always seem to offer too little, too late.

Government Responses to Major Bushfires

Victoria suffered drought conditions for the last decade, apparently broken during the unusually wet 2010-11 summer. Between 2000 and 2009 there were eleven major summer bushfires, mostly in February. Of these, the 2002–3 and 2006–7 fires have been the subject of reviews and reports (Department of Premier and Cabinet, 2003; Country Fire Authority, 2007; Ministerial Taskforce 2007) and for the 2009 ones there was a Royal Commission (Parliament of Victoria, op. cit.). In addition, in 2002 the Council of Australian Governments (COAG) commissioned a review of the way Australia deals with natural disasters, recommending the establishment of a Catastrophic Disasters Emergency Management Capability Working Group, and in 2004 conducted a national inquiry into bushfires following the 2002–3 fire season, which was particularly severe across south-eastern Australia. Both attempt to set nation-wide standards for prevention, protection and recovery. The 2004 review summary states:

> We have been learning to live with fire since the first Australians arrived on our continent. We need to continue, and enrich, that learning process in contemporary circumstances and be able to adapt our planning and responses to change. This report seeks to help all Australians meet these challenges.
>
> (Ellis, Kanowski and Whelan, 2004: 2)

The need to 'continue and enrich' is demonstrated in what the report calls the bushfire event and response cycle: Major bushfire event – Growing complacency – Accusations and blame – Coronial inquiry and further consequences – Government or independent inquiry and consequences – Initial community compliance – Increase in emergency service funding (Kanowski, Whelan and Ellis, 2005: 78).

Going back to the horrendous Black Friday fires of 1939, eleven common themes emerge from all the Australian bushfire inquiries: increased emphasis on risk reduction; the value of volunteers; education and awareness; complacency; the adequacy of resourcing; protective burning; communication; the importance of access; local knowledge; local government; and the insurance industry. Therefore 'breaking the cycle of institutional and individual response' is perhaps the 'greatest national challenge in mitigating the impacts of bushfires' (op. cit.). The related national inquiry gives education an important role in that task.

Most reports following major fires in Victoria have focused, however, on three themes: recovery after fires with a major emphasis on relief and rebuilding; future prevention through environmental measures and individual and community preparedness; and the responsiveness and coordination of responsible agencies. When fire threatens, and in its aftermath, these are priorities, and not only does it take time to rebuild damaged property, but damaged lives may take even longer to heal (Mental Health Research and Evaluation Centre, South Australian Health Commission, 1985). It is the second theme, prevention, which is the major subject of this chapter. Given the repeated stress throughout the last decade in this role of communities, it is important to look at both formal and non-formal education.

A Ministerial Taskforce was established after the 2002–3 Victorian fires to assess their impact. It provided the direct antecedent for the current approach. The three state fire agencies (DSE, CFA and MFB) developed *Fire Ready Victoria 2004–2007*, a three-year strategy for delivering bushfire information and education programmes throughout Victoria. Now joined by the Department of Human Services for a 'more coordinated approach to delivering services across the Prevention, Preparedness, Response and Recovery (PPRR) continuum', the 2008–12 *Living with Fire* strategy is sub-titled 'A Community Engagement Framework' (CFA/MFB/Victoria, 2008). The four partner agencies have both a 'legislative responsibility for fire management and a commitment to promote community well-being in relation to fire in Victoria' (ibid.: 4).

The 2006 Ministerial Taskforce claimed that measures put in place following its Report and one by the Auditor General (2003) created

> a spirit of cooperation that minimised individual tragedy and loss in the 2006 fires … other factors that reduced the loss of life and property were improvements in operational fire management, *the preparedness of local communities* and the high level of cooperation between local councils during and after the fires'. (Foreword; emphases added) Further, this was said to indicate 'the greater commitment of fire agencies to inform and involve local communities throughout fire suppression and recovery'.
> (Ministerial Taskforce, 2006)

A new Victorian Ministerial Taskforce on Bushfire Recovery was established in 2007. This time the Chair pointed out that

> Once again, the level of community engagement from a very early stage in the fire response was outstanding … Being prepared, equipped and confident,

> and simply knowing what to do as a fire approaches, has ensured that many Victorians and their assets in rural and remote communities have been able to survive the passage of wildfire … Central to the recovery package is almost $69 million in initiatives to ensure that communities are stronger and safer …
>
> (Ministerial Taskforce, 2007)

Building stronger and safer communities was therefore one of the recovery strategies nominated by the Taskforce, expressed in vague terms, especially regarding the partners to 'build leadership and training criteria into grants funding, and better link education, training and jobs programmes' (ibid., 36). The Director of Operations/Chief Fire Officer for the CFA, responding to the Operational Reviews of Major Fires in Victoria 2006/07 undertaken jointly for the DSE and the CFA, noted that community information flows had 'worked well' during that fire season. Sustainability of the information flows was nevertheless listed as a future priority requiring strategic action (Smith, 2007: 2). A tension emerges between allocating praise for changes introduced and actions taken, while revealing the need for greater and better efforts.

The most thorough review is the 2009 Victorian Bushfires Royal Commission. The Commission suggests demographic and climatic factors are likely to increase the risk of fires and their severity. Three demographic factors are particularly relevant: the growing population at the rural-urban interface 'where suburbs meet the bush' and where it is postulated that the risk of fires started by human action is increasing; anticipated population growth in a number of rural areas of Victoria where newcomers are likely to have very little, if any, bushfire awareness, and an increased proportion of older Victorians living in rural areas who may be bushfire-aware but not able to help themselves during a fire. Diverse and targeted approaches to bushfire prevention are required.

The Commission Report critiques existing information about and communication during bushfires, recommending new and more effective educational programmes. It calls for revision of bushfire safety measures. These require transmission to the community and a change of attitude by many householders. As a result of the high loss of life in 2009, there is greater emphasis on early evacuation on a high fire-risk day, rather than staying to defend property. There is also a repeatedly emphasised need for greater education about fire reduction burning prior to the fire season, an often controversial procedure.

How the recommendations of the Royal Commission have been aligned with the pre-existing *Living with Fire* strategy is not clear. Since the latter is more schematic than detailed, there should be no problems including the more specific recent recommendations about target groups and means. The overall strategy is based on a continuum with four identifiable phases for action: *preventative* actions throughout the year; *preparedness* for action when the summer fire season is approaching, involving designated agencies, communities and individuals; *response* when fire breaks out, and *recovery* after the danger has passed (the PPRR approach).

This approach includes the ongoing dissemination of information to residents, community development strategies to enhance knowledge of the role of fire and how to prevent disastrous ones, and community-agency-government partnerships to ensure ongoing involvement in the PPRR process. The Royal Commission in particular stresses an important role for schools. What is missing from the reports is any detailed consideration of and guide-lines for the role of formal education in bushfire prevention and preparedness. Many of the fires occur during the summer school holidays, though the danger season extends from spring into the new school year (late January or early February). Some of the most destructive Victorian fires have been in February.

Two of the 67 recommendations from the Royal Commission are specifically about education:

> Recommendation 2: The State revise the approach to community bushfire safety education in order to:
> - ensure that the publications and educational materials reflect the revised bushfire safety policy
> - equip all fire agency personnel with the information needed to effectively communicate the policy to the public as required
> - ensure that in content and delivery the programme is flexible enough to engage individuals, households and communities and to accommodate their needs and circumstances
> - regularly evaluate the effectiveness of community education programmes and amend them as necessary.
>
> Recommendation 6: Victoria lead an initiative of the Ministerial Council for Education, Early Childhood Development and Youth Affairs to ensure that the national curriculum incorporates the history of bushfire in Australia and that existing curriculum areas such as geography, science and environmental studies include elements of bushfire education.

The 2004 National Inquiry on Bushfire Mitigation and Management points out that although successive inquiries back as far as 1939 'have made recommendations relating to the central importance of bushfire education at both school and community levels' (op. cit.: 36), it is 'a matter of considerable concern that it remains necessary for this Inquiry to reiterate such recommendations' (ibid.: 37).

Education

A consistent theme in national reviews and inquiries into natural disasters is the need for improved information and warning systems, especially the delivery of clear, accurate information to communities. The distinction between the dissemination of information and education is sometimes blurred throughout the reviews and reports, and information dissemination acting as education is the most common approach. The 2009 Victorian Royal Commission deals separately with information and warnings. Warnings, together with safety instructions, are vital when fires are imminent or occurring, but will not be further considered in this chapter. However 'information' versus 'education' will be an ongoing theme.

The greatest emphasis on education is its delivery to communities. The focus is on promoting scrub clearing, controlling burning of bushland well before the hottest period of the year, preparing emergency personnel and emergency strategies, informing households about what to do before, during and after a fire, and helping communities and individuals in what may well be an extended recovery after a fire.

Education is not one of those government services actively involved in any of the above, and the state Department has not been represented on the various bodies developing strategies. As part of recovery processes counselling has been provided for school communities affected by fires. Otherwise, in contrast to other highly specific recommendations, education is simply added to this wish list of follow-up actions. As with so many new issues in society, it has become customary to refer the matter to schools, to do with it what they will, as if there is an 'education fix' for everything. Rather than asking why this has occurred, the more productive question is: what roles are there for education, both formal and non-formal, during bushfire prevention, preparedness, response and recovery?

A second question is: what sorts of approaches to education on this topic are appropriate in the different contexts in which it will take place? Many of the issues being addressed in the official strategy revolve around preventative actions that are most appropriately undertaken by adults. A clear role for work with children in both primary and secondary schools needs to be established.

What should be offered to all children in the state/nation, and what specifically for those in designated fire-prone areas? At what age should such education start? Should it address the four stages in the PPRR strategy and be delivered as a special 'package', or be framed in such a way that it can be taught across the curriculum? Something not addressed at all in any official documents is the preparation of current and future teachers to deliver bushfire education to pupils. And what about the education of the professionals involved in bushfire mitigation, management and recovery? This includes firefighters and emergency crews, police, health professionals and volunteers who respond to a fire outbreak.

The rest of this chapter deals separately with adult and community, school and professional education. Programmes and pedagogical issues will be considered and, where available, programme evaluations.

Bushfire Education for Adults: Informing the Public and Building Stronger Communities

There is a tension in the various reviews and reports between the dissemination of information about protection from bushfires on the one hand, and the broader concept of 'learning to live with fire' on the other, implying an educational process. The latter includes prevention and protection but also emphasises increasing people's understanding of the role of fire in the Australian environment and the need for action to reduce flammable bushland. Threading through both is the concept of building stronger communities to resist fires and to recover from their devastation. Shared responsibility between government and people to prevent fires is now an underlying motif and the prime rationale for community education.

Across Australia, fire agencies have been charged as the principal instigators of community fire education, awareness and engagement programmes. The Bushfire Co-operative Research Centre (BCRC) has undertaken an assessment of such programmes, and the Department of Justice also commissions evaluations. The programmes are defined as 'interventions intended to increase people's perception of their risk of bushfire and to generate changes in behaviour to reduce their bushfire risk' (Gilbert, 2007: 2). Information about local conditions and resources are central to them. Overall, the education programmes of the fire agencies 'mainly focus on prevention and preparedness measures that inform individual and community action both prior to the fire season and in response to an imminent fire threat. There are also programmes and activities that focus on providing timely and accurate information to communities when there is a fire and supporting communities during recovery from a fire' (ibid.). The largest number of such programmes was undertaken in Victoria (ten, followed by eight each for New South Wales and Western Australia).

The following activities take place: media campaigns, both interactive (CD-ROM) and printed publications, street and community meetings, community briefings during and after a fire, a dedicated telephone information line and a facilitated community development programme to establish local neighbourhood strategies. The CFA and DSE have a combined display for use in a variety of settings, including schools, largely as a marketing tool on the role of the DSE in bushfire prevention, and local fire brigades offer similar displays.

Media campaigns are mounted in late spring, mostly using short sharp advertisements for television, a technique successfully used for basic safety and health messages. Research indicates the type of message, the deliverer and the medium most likely to be trusted and to lead people to act on the advice (Walker et al., 2006; Strahan Research, 2007). Forty per cent of people in fire-prone areas listen to ABC and local radio for bushfire information, 35% would ring the local fire brigade and 34% would contact neighbours or friends. Local authorities such as the local CFA Brigade are most trusted as information sources, and in both studies the internet was a preferred source, especially by the under-50s. A potential problem arises since power supply is often an early victim during fires. Different age groups prefer different information sources, and there are some differences between men and women, and people from English-speaking and non-English-speaking backgrounds.

The main aim of most programmes is to increase people's understanding of fire, to activate people to prepare for fires and to work together especially when there is a fire emergency. There is a heavy emphasis on information transmission, especially through the distribution of pamphlets. Printed information has a role within a suite of preventative strategies for educating the general public. Provision of emergency phone numbers and listing media programmes to monitor are vital to enable people to obtain up-to-date details of fire conditions. The pamphlets also outline advice about fire-making plans and survival during a fire.

While it is a priority to inform people during a serious fire, the need to prepare people for a fire season is now acknowledged. A community safety approach has evolved nationally over the past decade, a shift from response and recovery to preparation (Elsworth et al., 2009: 6). In Victoria this is activated both through the *Fire Ready Victoria* programme which is based on information dissemination, and through *Community Fireguard*, the community development programme of the CFA.

Research in 2007 in fire-prone areas showed that 93.5% of respondents had received bushfire safety information from the local fire brigade, mostly through mail or letterbox drops (Strahan Research, op. cit.: 6). *Fire Ready* issued all households in the state in spring 2010 with a pamphlet entitled 'Prepare. Act. Survive', containing essential information for the fire season. It has updated information about total fire ban district boundaries, and the new emergency fire weather category (Code Red: the worst conditions for a bush or grass fire). In line with the Royal Commission recommendations, it also includes the advice that leaving high-risk bushfire areas the night before or early in the day is the safest option. Local government councils also distribute information leaflets to householders, especially in fire-prone municipalities.

The newest approach, *Community Fireguard*, invites communities to establish small local groups to develop strategies for themselves, with back-up facilitation and information. Following the 2009 fires, both programmes have been reviewed, since their application was seen as limited as it depends on voluntary attendance. Following the report of the Royal Commission, the number of meetings has increased to 887, with 337 new groups formed. This is still fewer meetings than envisaged in the functioning of the programme. The number of *Fire Ready* meetings has also increased (to 2197: Government of Victoria, 2011). Nearly all programmes rely on being 'homogenous in delivery across diverse communities' (Sturzenegger and Hayes, 2011: 57).

Perceptions of Risk and Communication in a Culturally Diverse Nation

Risk construction and communication are both complex. Communication about the risks is a central part of bushfire education even though it is now located within the wider context of the PPRR continuum. The social science literature asserts that risk is culturally embedded and its meaning socially constructed (Stallings, 1990). It is difficult to see a bushfire racing through the countryside fanned by 150kph winds on a 45°C midsummer day and not perceive it as a threat. As the danger passes, rain falls and a new season approaches; however, memories fade even in previously affected areas. It is at the point of preparation and prevention that different perceptions of the nature and degree of risk are likely to affect an individual's search for information, and willingness to engage in preparatory actions. Knowledge of how people perceive the risk thus forms a basis for effective communication about the risk and motivation for action. And a basic tenet of the provision of risk information asserts that it is not just a one-way transfer of information, nor is it a single discrete event. Thus, '[i]f risk communication is interactive, then those who would inform others about risk should take into account the concerns and priorities of the recipients of the information' (Fessenden-Raden et al., 1987: 94).

Some work has been done on perception of risk, and on attitudes to bushfire safety, including actions taken. Nevertheless, linking the two aspects, perception and actions, has not so far been undertaken. The most relevant study was commissioned for the Country Fire Authority prior to the 2007/2008 summer season (Strahan Research, 2007). It surveyed 1024 respondents in four high bushfire risk locations. People were asked about their participation in bushfire safety meetings, opinions about specific dangers during a fire, bushfire safety measures undertaken, what actions they were most likely to take if a bushfire occurred near them, whether they had a fire plan and how prepared they were to implement it, and in what ways they would get information when a bushfire broke out. The study revealed that 'a significant proportion of respondents have not adequately planned how to respond' (p. 8) and significant numbers of respondents had had little involvement in bushfire safety meetings. Nor had many adopted important measures to protect property during a fire. Their perception of bushfire risk can only be inferred from the actions they did or did not take, though another study found it was considered the greatest of six environmental hazards (Burns et al., 2010).

The need to acknowledge population diversity recurs in recent literature about bushfire preparedness (Fien, 2009) and in actions taken to implement the Royal Commission recommendations. Diversity includes people from different cultural backgrounds, different ages, varied prior experiences with bushfire and people with disabilities. Messages are more effective when they are strategically matched to audience needs, values, background, culture and experiences (Reynolds and Seeger, 2005). This again points to the need for communication to be an interactive process. Updated information distributed to the community in Victoria post-2009 recognises this.

Recognition of the need for diverse approaches raises the issue of the link between education and warnings. Both the communication chain which links emergency preparedness to emergency outbreaks (Betts, n.d.) and the actual warnings themselves have been inadequate during past emergencies (Handmer, 2000–2). The Royal Commission report points out that '[t]he success of specific bushfire warnings partly depends on the standard of the information *and education provided to the community prior to its issue*' [emphasis added] (Parliament of Victoria, 2010: 120).

A specific at-risk group during a fire is out-of-area visitors, unfamiliar with local conditions and facilities. This is particularly pertinent as most fires occur during the summer holiday period. A pamphlet supported by the Royal Automobile Club of Victoria provides specific advice to those who are travelling during the bushfire season, both to secure the home before leaving and if encountering fire while travelling. Information about fire safety has also been directed at the tourist industry.

Bushfire information and education has increased over the past decade, and is now a major strategy in the prevention of and preparation for bushfires by both Commonwealth and State governments. The Commonwealth Attorney-General's Department sponsors a range of national programmes and activities to engage communities in building resilience to the effects of emergencies and disasters, especially through the initiatives of the Australian Emergency Management Institute. In Victoria there has been a Fire Communications Taskforce since 2005, established by the Department of Justice, to undertake a whole government approach to community education and communication about fires. The Department of Sustainability and Environment's 'Living with Fire – a Community Engagement Framework' brings together the DSE, CFA, MFB and DHS to develop a coordinated approach to the delivery of education and engagement across the state.

Psychological and Pedagogical Considerations

There is a tension underlying bushfire education programmes between the 'empowerment' and 'behaviour change' approaches, also found in the literature on disaster education, including bushfires. Research suggests that behaviour change is a common goal throughout programmes, the difference being in the educational approach to this. Behaviour change, at least relating to intended protective behaviours, is easier to evaluate than empowerment, a more general concept and related mostly to community development. A promising approach to motivating behaviour change comes from research on resilience and coping in individuals. The application to the initiation of preventative actions and to survival after a major disaster has been limited. An interview study of survivors of the 2009 Victorian bushfires provides insight into the experiences of 33 survivors who faced extreme danger. Control over their fear and maintenance of attention on the major threats to life and their implications for action were the key strategies employed by these 'deep' survivors (McLennan et al., 2011). These behaviours may define fire-resilient people.

Psychological research contributes to ways to motivate people to deal with hazards such as bushfires. A series of studies in New Zealand and the US examined both children's and adults' understanding of natural hazards and preparedness for them, and the effectiveness of interventions to promote disaster coping. They found that it is possible to raise levels of knowledge about and awareness of hazards but that this does not necessarily translate into better preparedness (Johnston et al., 2005; Ronan et al., 2008). This was also found in the Strahan study of bushfire preparedness in Victoria. A social-cognitive hazard preparation model would include the motivators or precursors, intention formation, and moderators of the intention-preparedness link. Such studies highlight the role of individual psychological characteristics such as belief in self-efficacy as a contributor to intentions, perceived responsibility and sense of community.

Applied social psychology may offer insights, as suggested by Beatson and McLennan (2011) in their exploration of links between health promotion strategies and improving community bushfire safety. How improving individual preparedness contributes to community resilience and how to implement the Victorian 'self-reliant communities' strategic direction of 2002–5 remain largely wishful thinking. At best, it relies on creating partnerships, engaging communities and delivering programmes about risk management. It is assumed that this will empower communities with the knowledge, skills and resources needed to manage their own fire safety. Translating ideas into practice requires a greater investment in research and development than is presently available.

Educating Children and Young People about Bushfires

Before considering bushfire education programmes in schools, it is pertinent to ask if this is a worthwhile activity, given limited roles for children during a fire, and the ever-increasing demands on teachers and the curriculum.

Can We Educate Children about Bushfires?

In studies of young people and hazards education, researchers have found that hazard education programmes can be effective in increasing hazard awareness, more realistic risk perceptions, more knowledge of risk mitigation, and increased levels of home-based hazard adjustments as children discuss their schoolwork with parents (Ronan and Johnston, 2001). The studies consistently show that while civil defence education can increase knowledge and awareness, there is a gap between this and preparedness for action, in part related to the time gap between the receipt of education and the appearance or likelihood of the hazardous event (Finnis et al., 2010). Arguing that effective hazard education will increase individual and community resilience to disasters and their consequences, they have investigated ways to improve the effectiveness of preventative interventions.

Studies in New Zealand have assessed children's current beliefs about particular hazards, levels of preparedness and levels of emotional functioning before and after a hazards education intervention. They have found that children's participation in such a programme increases accurate hazards knowledge, decreases inaccurate knowledge, increases reports of home adjustments relating to the hazard, and leads to more realistic risk perceptions (Ronan et al., 2008). The number of programmes children are exposed to, their recency and their content are all factors that affect programme effectiveness in bringing about increased knowledge, awareness and emotional coping. Educational programmes about hazards for children are effective especially if they take findings about content into account. In particular, specific information about emergency management procedures had a significantly greater impact on children's hazard-related awareness, knowledge, and the number of hazard adjustments adopted in the household (Ronan and Johnston, 2003).

In addition to the specific benefits to children of hazards education, both cognitive and emotional, it has also been found to increase home-based adjustments for hazards, through:

- increased interaction between children and parents about hazards programmes
- specific knowledge of emergency management procedures
- multiple education programme involvement
- more recent education programme involvement. (Ronan et al., 2008: 344)

Recent research on Australian children's knowledge of the risk of bushfires addresses a serious gap in understanding children's conceptualisations of 'risk', 'hazard' and 'disaster', especially in relation to bushfires. Towers (2011) points out that effective education must accommodate children's knowledge and perspectives, as a basis for the development of educational programmes and materials. Her work has shown that children's knowledge of bushfire risk is based on their participation in their communities in discussion and actions about bushfire risk-reduction, and their own processes of constructing meaning.

Not only do children learn about hazards through their socio-cultural interactions; educating children about hazards is an effective way to engage households and communities. Further, younger children are better communicators with adults about these issues than teenagers, through such means as discussion-directed homework tasks. The benefits include increased physical preparedness and emotional readiness (Ronan et al., 2008). To add a cautionary note, it is not sufficient to have the 'right' content; there should be evaluation and documented effectiveness, in particular to see if there have been improvements in the preparedness of families and individuals following an educational intervention (Ronan et al., 2010).

Bushfire Education in Schools

The above researchers suggest it would be beneficial to extend the network of school-youth-family to the wider community especially through linking schools with emergency management agencies. Such links are used in bushfire education in Australia. The Commonwealth Attorney-General's Department has funded a major national project on hazards education for primary school children, carried out by the Australasian Fire and Emergency Services Authorities Council (AFAC). AFAC continues to work with the Victorian CFA in the production of bushfire-specific materials for children and teachers. In addition to the national materials development by AFAC, state fire authorities have developed materials in each state and go into schools to deliver their messages.

There is a diversity of educational material suppliers, with the causes and effects of fires a major theme in all the materials. The Victorian CFA is a major player in providing materials and speakers for schools. (A point worth stressing here is that it is important to ensure that agency speakers involved in schools have some pedagogical training to enhance their delivery.) The Attorney-General's Department's Emergency Management for Schools programme has a bushfire web page suggesting projects around the causes of bushfires, their devastation to communities, how to survive during a bushfire and how to prepare better for a bushfire. The Red Cross is concerned with post-disaster recovery rather than prevention and preparation, and has a brochure for use at that time with parents and young children. The state Department of Sustainability and Environment (DSE) produces online material on bushfires, largely on causes of bushfires in Victoria, how DSE fights fires and how fire affects the environment. They produce publications on bushfire safety and on their planned burns programme. Other examples include the Victorian National Parks Association factsheets for schools on the History of Fire in Australia, and a series of questions and answers on the 2009 Victorian fires. The National Museum has material on Fire in Australia suitable for Years 9–12, with suggestions as to where it fits into investigation projects in geography, studies of society and environment or indigenous studies. And Zoos Victoria produced an imaginative Bushfires and Wildlife Challenge for students on ways to improve biodiversity and reduce fire risk in the community, which includes tasks for children and a teachers' toolbox. State teachers are seconded to work in the general educational programmes of Zoos Victoria; cooperation between organisation and educational personnel for the other materials is not clear.

Many of these materials, interesting and attractive as they are, are simply 'out there' for teachers to find and use as they see fit. As any educational researcher knows, the more teachers are assisted to use materials through sample lesson plans and examples of use in different curriculum areas, the more likely they are to be adopted. It is therefore encouraging to see that the research undertaken by Briony Towers into children's knowledge and understanding of bushfires and bushfire risk has been translated into television safety messages and this is now being further developed with teacher resource back-up for use in the 5–12 age group, with specific suggestions for different age groupings of children. Short animated 'L'il Safety Club' messages aimed to dispel misconception, provide information in children's words and call to action, based on children's perspectives elicited through research, are presented (Towers et al., 2010; AFAC, 2011). Teacher support materials are provided and the current work with the CFA is intended for use within the new Australian Curriculum for all Australian schools, which is still being developed (the curriculum for the first eleven years for English, mathematics, science and history was published in 2010).

In response to the 2009 Bushfires Royal Commission Recommendation 2, the state Department of Education and Early Childhood Development, through Education Services Australia, and supported by the Victorian Curriculum and Assessment Authority's Bushfire Working Party, has developed materials for the first eleven years of schooling. A Bushfire Education website provides resources for both learners and teachers. The framework is the current three learning domains (physical, personal and social learning, discipline-based learning, and interdisciplinary learning) and the essential learning standards framework (VELS), introduced into the state in 2006. Four modules have been developed, around the themes: learning about bushfires, preparing for bushfires, responding to bushfires and recovering from bushfires. There is also a fifth theme, 'bringing it together', designed to help learners integrate what they have learnt and suggest ways they could put their new knowledge into practice (Department of Education and Early Childhood Development, 2011). Each module is designed for use either as a sequential programme for cross-curricular learning or as individual topics for insertion into existing key learning areas.

The new resources sit side-by-side with the extensive CFA programme, *Fire Safe Kids* (CFA, 2011). This includes resources and manuals for teachers and workbooks and resources for students, with a detailed breakdown for levels 1–6 of the VELS. In 2011 it replaced their programme, *Brigades in Schools*, and is available free in fire-prone areas. It includes presentations by CFA members, trained to work in schools. Each presentation is for one period with one class. Suggested activities and lesson plans for pre-and post-visit sessions are also provided.

Until the national curriculum is in place, it is the task of each state's education authorities to provide the framework for school curricula. Each school and within that each teacher is responsible for the daily curriculum and choice of materials. The emphasis in overall bushfire emergency management and mitigation on the need for diversity, Towers' findings on the role of children's socio-cultural environment in shaping their bushfire knowledge, and the demonstration of Ronan et al. that context is a relevant variable in hazards education and preparedness for action, validate continuing localised adaptations in approaches with children. The diversity of students (e.g. those with special needs, or still learning English) is not specifically mentioned. And while the Victorian bushfire education website has links to material specifically for teenagers, further details on how or why they may need different approaches, indicated by Shean's research (2011), is lacking. With a growing list of resources, and ever-increasing pressures on teachers, what will be delivered in specific classrooms? Is evaluation taking place? And who is in-servicing teachers to chart their way through both the materials and their application in different classrooms?

Schools, Education and the Trauma of Bushfires

Alongside the general direction of bushfire education in schools, with its emphasis on increased knowledge and preparedness to act, the research findings on the need for enhanced problem-solving and coping skills is underrepresented in the materials. However, there is a separate set of educational resources especially designed for use in schools in areas recently affected by fires. The AFAC project materials feed directly into that. And Victoria has recently released a booklet for use with families of young children, 'Here for Each Other', produced by the US TV programme 'Sesame Street'. The Red Cross has produced its own book for parents, guardians, carers and teachers to help kids cope with emergencies, 'After the Emergency'. The Australian Child and Adolescent Trauma, Loss and Grief Network and the Australian National University established a Children's Futures: Positive Strategies for Bushfire Recovery resource web page after the 2009 fires for use Australia-wide, and with the Australian Psychological Society, a brochure on the same topic. The Victorian Education Department has its own page of support resources for children, including what to do on fire anniversaries.

An example of supportive action at the school level is seen in the activities of one primary school where there was considerable loss of life in the February 2009 fires. A 'school ace' programme rewards children who exemplify the school values, with winners announced in the weekly newsletter, which feeds into community development goals. There was a money-raising event for the CFA and improved fire safety works to school buildings and grounds. Recognising the lasting effects of fire trauma for some people, a parent infor-mation session was held almost two years after the fires with staff from the Monash University Psychological Recovery Unit. This is a good example of a school as a centre for community fire education and community development.

Given that school-aged children's parents are often the hardest to reach by other means with bushfire information (Walker et al.), this role for schools has been underplayed in most of the literature and programmes.

At the most basic point of bushfires and education, there are bushfire preparedness guidelines for schools, another initiative arising out of the 2009 Bushfire Royal Commission. They are concerned with the safety of both students and school property – teachers are not mentioned! Compliance is required for a school to be registered to operate.

Further and Professional Education

The Bushfire Co-operative Research Centre is a leading centre for research into diverse aspects of bushfires, and links universities, agencies and government instrumentalities and departments. At present its educational side offers scholarships for higher degree students, and also provides a detailed rationale and framework for courses teaching about aspects of fire across the higher education spectrum.

Among the professions, psychologists have been active in providing information and both as individuals and as teams, undertaking research into resilience, coping and trauma recovery and the application of psychological research to education. In October 2010, to mark UN International Disaster Reduction Day, their professional organisation, the APS, announced the establishment of a website to help combat the trauma of natural disasters. It is a joint initiative of the APS, the Australian Centre for Posttraumatic Mental Health, Occupational Therapy Australia, the Royal Australian and New Zealand College of Psychiatrists, the Australian Association of Social Workers, the Royal Australian College of General Practitioners and General Practice Victoria.

In 2001 the Victorian State Trauma Committee developed a Trauma Education Framework for the education and training of all [health professional] staff involved in trauma care, including the aftermath of fires. It is designed for undergraduate, postgraduate and continuing education but does not include implementation guidelines. There is a special emphasis on a curriculum for disaster medicine. Gender issues in bushfires and natural disasters generally, and for training of professionals for this, have been raised by Women's Health Victoria and arising from recent research (Eriksen et. al., 2010).

The CFA, MFB, SES and Police have their own training programmes.

The CFA has conducted training and briefing sessions in the lead up to and during the 2009–10 bushfire season, especially about the changed approaches to community communications and alterations to the 'stay or go' policy. AFAC has a detailed recommendation for ongoing accreditation of command and control personnel as well as all those involved in emergency services. They suggest a hierarchy of qualifications within the Technical and Further Education (TAFE) framework from Level 2 Certificates through Levels 3 and 4 and on to the Diploma in Public Safety (firefighting management) and the Advanced Diploma in the same field. There is no overall policy regarding bushfire education within professional development for teachers at any level.

Media education is needed about their reporting on bushfires (Muller & Gawenda, 2011) and on emergencies in general (Walker et al., 2006). People rely heavily on the media for information about emergencies, while being selective about their preferred information sources, and realise the inadequacy of some media messages during a fire.

Conclusion

The foregoing has focused on the role of education in bushfire management and mitigation. As policies have shifted from preparation and recovery to prevention, preparedness, response and recovery, with community development and government-agency-community partnerships as key factors, the role of education has been emphasised. This is leading to the development of resource materials at all levels. Questions remain concerning the major goals of bushfire education, especially between empowerment and behaviour change emphases, the effectiveness of programme delivery, the recognition of population diversity in educational approaches, and the role of research in establishing educational objectives, approaches and evaluations.

Acknowledgments

Grateful thanks are offered to Amanda Leck (AFAC), Jim McLennan (Bushfire CRC), Kevin Ronan (Central Queensland University) and Briony Towers (University of Tasmania) for their generous responses to inquiries about their research, copies of papers and discussion of issues.

Questions for Further Consideration

1. What roles are there for education, both formal and non-formal, during bushfire prevention, preparedness, response and recovery? What do you suggest in addition to those considered in this chapter?
2. Accepting the prevent, prepare, respond, recover continuum, how would you approach teaching these issues in a bushfire-prone school (either primary/elementary, or post-primary)? Consider a specialised unit versus across-the-curriculum approach.
3. How would you set up a community development programme for strengthening a community's ability to deal with bushfires?

Suggestions for Further Reading

Many of the materials covered in this chapter can be readily accessed online from the appropriate government department or agency website, as named in the text, including teaching resources. The ground-breaking research by Briony Towers linking chidren's knowledge of risks to educational programmes will soon be available as she has very recently completed her doctorate on it at the University of Tasmania. In the two areas, adult and community, and in-school education, I have elected to highlight two references for each; for the latter, teaching resources are selected. Readers are also urged to consult the relevant sections of the Royal Commission Report into the 2009 Victorian Bushfires, especially Volume II. Accessible at: www.royalcommission.vic.gov.au/Commission-Reports/Final-Report.

Adult and Community Education

Fien, J. (2009) *Evaluating Bushfire Community Education Programs. Final Report: Project C7*. Melbourne: RMIT University. This report of extensive research provides an excellent overview and evaluation of all the main community education projects about bushfire that have been conducted in Australia in the last decade.

Sturzenegger, L. and Hayes, T. (2011) Post Black Saturday: development of a bushfire safety system, *Australian Journal of Emergency Management* 26(2): 54–9. This article provides a succinct overview of the current Victorian official approach to creating safer communities, to strengthen resilience to bushfire and reduce its risk.

In-School Education

Department of Education and Early Childhood Development (2011) Bushfire Education. www.bushfireeducation./vic.edu.au/about-this-resource.html [Accessed 15 September 2011]. This is the portal for the full materials for P-10, as described in the foregoing text.

CFA (2011) *Fire Safe Kids*. In addition to pamphlets, see: www.cfa.vic.gov.au/firesafety/educationandtraining/firesafekids.htm [Accessed 14 September 2011]. These resources cover teaching materials, teacher notes, suggested activities and a guide to the way in which the material could be included across the Victorian Essential Learning Standards (VELS).

References

AFAC (2011). *Natural Hazards Children's Program*. Melbourne: AFAC (Teachers' resource DVD).

Beatson, R. and McLennan, J. (2011). What applied social psychology theories might contribute to community bushfire safety research after Victoria's 'Black Saturday'. *Australian Psychologist* 46, 3, 171–82.

Betts, R. (undated). *The Missing Links in Community Warning Systems*. Melbourne: Office of the Emergency Services Commissioner, Victoria.

Burns, R., Robinson, P. and Smith, P. (2010). From hypothetical scenario to tragic reality: A salutary lesson in risk communication and the Victorian 2009 bushfires, *Australian and New Zealand Journal of Public Health*, 34, 1, 24–31.

CFA (undated). Major Fires www.cfa.vic.gov.au/about/historymajorfires..htm [Accessed 30 August 2011].

CFA/MFB/Victoria [DSE and DHS] (2008). *Living with Fire. A Community Engagement Framework 2008–2012*. Melbourne: Government Printer for the State of Victoria. See also www.cfa.vic.gov.au/publications/bushfireStrategy.htm [Accessed 30 August 2011].

Country Fire Authority (2007). *Key Issues Identified from Operational Reviews of Major Fires in Victoria 2006/07*. Melbourne: CFA.

CSIRO (2008). *Bushfire in Australia*. Available at: www/csiro.au/resources/BushfireInAustralia.html [Accessed 17 August 2011].

Department of Premier and Cabinet (2003). *Inquiry into the 2002–2003 Victorian Bushfires*. Melbourne: Government Printer for the State of Victoria.

Ellis, S., Kanowski, P. and Whelan, R. (2004). *National Inquiry on Bushfire Mitigation and Management*. Canberra: Commonwealth of Australia.

Elsworth, G., Gilbert, J., Rhodes, A. and Goodman, H. (2009). Community safety programs for bushfire: What do they achieve, and how? *Australian Journal of Emergency Management* 24, 2, 17–25.

Eriksen, C., Gill, N. and Head, L. (2010). The gendered dimensions of bushfire in changing rural landscapes in Australia. *Journal of Rural Studies*, 26, 332–42.

Fessenden-Raden, J., Fitchen, J. M. and Heath, J. S. (1987). Providing risk information in communities: factors influencing what is heard and accepted. *Science, Technology and Human Values* 1, 2, 3 & 4, 94–101.

Finnis, K., Johnston, D., Ronan, K. and White, J. D. (2010). Hazard perceptions and preparedness of Tananaki youth. *Disaster Prevention and Management*, 19, 2, 175–84.

Gilbert, J. (2007). *Community Education, Awareness and Engagement Program for Bushfire: An Initial Assessment of Practices Across Australia.* Melbourne: Bushfire Cooperative Research Centre and School of Global Studies, Social Science & Planning, RMIT University.

Government of Victoria (2011). *Implementing the Government's response to the 2009 Victorian Bushfires Royal Commission.* Available at: www.cfa.vic.gov.au/documents/royal_commission_implementation_plan.pdf [Accessed 21 October 2011].

Handmer, J. (2000–2). Are flood warnings futile? Risk communication in emergencies. *The Australian Journal of Disaster and Trauma Studies.* Available at: www.massy.ac.nz/~trauma/issues/2000-2/handmer.htm [Accessed 30 August 2011].

Johnston, D., Paton, D., Crawford, G. L., Ronan, K., Houghton, B. and Bürgelt, P. (2005). Measuring tsunami preparedness in coastal Washington, United States. *Natural Hazards,* 35, 173–84.

Kanowski, P. J., Whelan, R. J. and Ellis, S. (2005). Inquiries following the 2002–2003 Australian bushfires: common themes and future directions for Australian bushfire mitigation and management. *Australian Forestry,* 68, 2, 76–86.

McLennan, J., Omodei, M., Elliott, G. and Holgate, A. (2011). 'Deep Survival': Experiences of some who lived when they might have died in the 7 February 2009 Bushfires. *Australian Journal of Emergency Management,* 26, 2, 41–6.

Mental Health Research and Evaluation Centre, South Australian Health Commission (1985). *The Health and Social Impact of the Ash Wednesday Bushfires.* Adelaide, Mental Health Research and Evaluation Centre.

Ministerial Taskforce on Bushfire Recovery (2006). *Report.* Melbourne: Government Printer for the State of Victoria.

—(2007). *Report.* Melbourne: Government Printer for the State of Victoria.

Muller, D. and Gawenda, M. (2011). *Black Saturday: In the Media Spotlight.* Parkville, Vic., Melbourne University Press.

Parliament of Victoria (2010). *Fire Preparation, Response and Recovery. Final Report, Volume II.* Melbourne: Government Printer of the State of Victoria.

Reynolds, B. and Seeger, M. W. (2005). Crisis and emergency risk communication as an integrative model. *Journal of Health Communication,* 10, 43–55.

Ronan, K. R., Crellin, K. and Johnston, D. (2010). Correlates of hazards education for youth: a replication study. *Natural Hazards,* 53, 3, 503–26.

Ronan, K. R., Crellin, K., Johnston, D. M., Finnis, K., Paton, D. and Becker, J. (2008). Promoting child and family resilience to disasters: effects, interventions, and prevention effectiveness. *Children, Youth and Environments* 18, 1, 332–53.

Ronan, K. R. and Johnston, D. M. (2001). Correlates of hazard education programs for youth. *Risk Analysis,* 21, 6, 1055–63.

—(2003). Hazards education for youth: a quasi-experimental investigation. *Risk Analysis*, 23, 5, 1009–20.

Shean, M. B. (2011). Resilience in Western Australian adolescents: processes that occur after the experience of risk. *Australian Community Psychologist*, 23, 2, 85–102.

Smith, R. (2007). *Key Issues Identified from Operational Reviews*. Melbourne: DSE and CFA.

Stallings, R. A. (1990). Media discourse and the social construction of risk. *Social* Problems, 37, 1, 80–95.

Strahan Research (2007). *Research for the Victorian Country Fire Authority on Community Attitudes to Bushfire Safety prior to the 2007/2008 Summer Season*. Melbourne: Strahan Research. Available at: www.strahan-research.com [Accessed 30 August 2011].

Towers, B. (2011). *Australian Children's Knowledge of Wildfire Risk*. Poster presented at the 36th Annual Natural Hazards Research and Applications Workshop, Broomfield, Colorado.

Towers, B., Paton, D. and Haynes, K. (2010). *Putting Research into Practice: Developing Bushfire Safety Messages for Children*. Poster presented at the AFAC and Bushfire CRC Conference, Sydney.

Walker, R., Robinson, P., Tebbutt, J., Lin, V., Burns, R. and Schauble, J. (2006). *Emergency Mangement Risk Communication Project. Final report to the Department of Human Services*. Victoria: School of Public Health, La Trobe University.

3 Natural Hazards in India: Forewarned is Forearmed

Colin Bangay

Chapter Outline

Introduction

From the earliest times humans have concentrated where the bounty of nature is most abundant. Coastal zones, river valleys, rich volcanic soils and fault lines where tectonic forces have brought mineral wealth and water within access have all attracted ever-increasing population densities. However, the very forces that deliver these resources can also devastate human societies. Flood, drought, earthquakes, tsunamis and volcanic eruptions have played an integral part in shaping early human history. Over time, advances in technology have enabled humankind to manipulate environments, enabling both rising populations and ever-higher levels of population density. The pace of this change has accelerated dramatically in the last 150 years during which the global population has shifted eightfold, from 1.26 billion to some seven billion (UN, 1999). The exponential growth of human population has been enabled through the harnessing of fossil fuels. This has led to a dramatic rise in atmospheric CO_2 levels that can be traced to the onset of the industrial revolution. The combined consequence of these twin and interconnected phenomena – fossil fuel use and population growth – is that the human race is no longer solely influenced by forces of nature. It is altering them. Nowhere is this more apparent than in India.

This chapter takes a two-part look at the role of education in the human relationship with the geophysical world in the subcontinent. The first part provides a contextual overview of hazards and disaster risk reduction (DRR) and the contribution of education to this in India. The second touches briefly on the emerging issues of climate change and population growth. It is concluded that there is great scope for integrating DRR and environmental education initiatives. However, to maximise the impact of such initiatives, greater attention must be paid to the broader education context – in particular low learning levels and the migration of students to the non-state sector. These realities need to inform both approach and targeting. Without this, and a more robust evidence base, endeavours will remain peripheral – the concern of dedicated but marginalised special interest groups.

Context: India Natural Hazards and Human Disasters – Past and Future

India is vulnerable to the majority of natural hazards with the exception of volcanoes. The Government of India's (GoI) National Disaster Management Authority estimates 58.6% of India's landmass (mainly the Himalayan region of north and north-east India) is prone to earthquakes of moderate to very high density. A further 12% of land area is prone to floods and river erosion (predominantly the north-eastern region). Furthermore, 68% of cultivable area is vulnerable to drought (mainly the north-western portion of the country) with hilly areas at risk from landslides. Of the 7,516 km. of coastline, close to 5,700 km. (the whole of the east coast and the Gujarat coast on the west) is vulnerable to cyclones and tsunamis (GoI, 2009). The coastline includes 18 cities of over one million people and it is estimated that the total population living along it is as high as 100 million (TERI, 2010).

The combination of geographical location and geological/seismic realities and climatic conditions make India particularly vulnerable to natural hazards. This is evident from prehistory: with flood, drought, tectonic uplift and ecological devastation all having been postulated to explain the demise of Indus valley civilisation (Kostman, 1996) to the present day devastation caused by the 2011 Sikkim earthquake and Orissa floods. India is assessed as the second most vulnerable country to natural disasters after China (Indian Express, 2011c). As a disaster-risk profile notes: 'both the multi-hazard mortality and GDP maps demonstrate that almost the entire country is significantly impacted by at least one hazard and mortality impacts are particularly concentrated in the north and north-eastern regions' (Columbia University, 2005).

A review of historic data over the last thirty years (EM-DAT, 2011), shows that weather and climatic events – cyclones, floods and droughts – are India's most common natural hazards. These impact on the largest number of people and within the given period have resulted in the highest economic losses (ibid). However, it is earthquakes and tsunamis that are associated with the highest levels of mortality (ibid.). Mercifully, severe earthquakes do not occur with the frequency with which India experiences drought and flood. However, a severe earthquake striking an area of high population density would have devastating consequences. India's rapid urbanisation and the fact that thirty-eight of India's major cities – including Delhi, Mumbai, Chennai and Kolkata – are located within seismic zones (Indian Express, 2010), makes this an inevitability at some point in the future.

Looking to the future, India faces ever-increasing disaster risk because of its expanding population, rapid urbanisation, development within high-risk zones, environmental degradation and exposure to climate change. The latest census data set India's population at 1.2 billion (GoI, 2011b), equivalent to the world population of 150 years ago (UN, 1999) or the combined populations of current day USA, Indonesia, Brazil, Pakistan, Bangladesh and Japan. India is also urbanising rapidly and is projected to experience a 'rural-urban transformation' as its urban population rises from 300 million to over 700 million by 2050, with an estimated 70 cities expected to reach populations of over one million in the next fifteen years (TERI, 2010). The combination of population growth and urbanisation contribute to India being ranked second in the World Climate Change Vulnerability Index 2011 (New Scientist, 2010). The Climate Change Vulnerability Index (CCVI), released by global risks advisory firm Maplecroft, states of India:

Almost the whole of India has a high or extreme degree of sensitivity to climate change, due to acute population pressure and a consequential strain on natural resources. This is compounded by a high degree of poverty, poor general health and the agricultural dependency of much of the populace.

(Maplecroft, 2010)

It is clear that the combination of population growth, climate change and the geophysical realities of India's location will mean that large-scale disaster events are going to feature in the lives of upcoming generations. It is therefore imperative both that the process of education is made as safe as possible (i.e. buildings, emergency drills and preparation) and that the education received equips students to better appreciate and respond better to environmental risks and climate change.

The Indian National Disaster Management System

Before looking at education-specific responses to disaster reduction, an overview of national disaster management is provided. This is in order that the reader can situate initiatives into the broader context.

India's vulnerability to disasters and the large-scale human and economic losses they cause has prompted the Indian government to invest significant effort in developing disaster preparedness and resilience. A clear shift has occurred over the last ten years. Disaster management has evolved from a predominantly reactive and 'relief-centric' focus to an approach in which natural hazard and disaster management is integrated into the broader development effort, the objective being the creation of prepared and disaster-resilient communities at all levels of society. This new approach takes a systematic 'before, during and after' perspective including strategies and provision around mitigation, preparedness, response, relief and rehabilitation.

The legal underpinning for India's disaster response is contained within the Disaster Management Act (GoI, 2005) and the Disaster Management Policy (GoI, 2009). The Disaster Management Act saw the creation of a tiered set of interlinked disaster management authorities reflecting India's federal system. The National Disaster Management Authority (NDMA) is the apex body mandated to lay down the policies, plans and guidelines. The NDMA is chaired by the prime minister, with a vice-chair and eight ministers all with particular briefs on specific hazard risks as well as oversight on levels of preparedness in specific states and union territories. Beneath this are the State Disaster Management Authorities (SDMA) headed by state chief ministers, and below these the District Disaster Management Authorities charged with planning, management, coordination and implementation of plans. Supporting the implementation of the Disaster Management Authorities are: (i) the National Institute of Disaster Management (NIDM), which undertakes research, capacity-building and policy advocacy; and (ii) the National Disaster Response Force, with ten battalions comprising 144 specialised teams trained to respond to natural and man-made events.

In addition to the institutional and governance structures detailed above, the Indian government has also made financial provision through the National and State Disaster Response funds. These are projected to total 33580.93 crore rupees ($4.6 billion) by 2014–15 (GoI, 2011a). Financing is organised on a 75:25% share for the majority of states and a 90:10 share for special category northeastern states. This financing is provided to support the preparation of state and district disaster management plans, the establishment of emergency operation centres (EoCs), strengthening fire and emergency services, and ensuring putting in place school safety programmes.

The work of the NDMA and NIDM is further supported by the Indian Meteorological Department, responsible for cyclone forecasting, and the Indian National Centre for Ocean Information Services, which houses India's newly inaugurated tsunami warning centre (Indian Express, 2011b). Important work has also been done on hazard maps that capture the spatial and temporal aspects of natural events along with the magnitude of impact. Of particular note are: the 'Natural Hazard Map of India', published by the National Atlas and Thematic Organisation (NATMO); the 'Vulnerability Atlas of India', produced by the Building Materials & Technology Promotion Council (BMTPC), which looks at infrastructure vulnerability; and the Seismic Map of India, prepared by the Bureau of Indian Standards (BIS), which categorises India into five zones according to seismic risk.

Augmenting the efforts of the GoI around disaster mitigation has been the work of the donor partners and non-government and civil society organisations. Given the scale of India and the localised nature of much of this work, it is practical here to highlight only two of the larger initiatives by way of example. Launched in 2002, the GoI UNDP Disaster risk Management Programme is one of the largest community based disaster risk management programmes in Asia. The programme is in operation in 17 states and 169 of India's most hazard-prone districts (UNDP, 2010). Key elements of the programme included integrating disaster management into the school curriculum, educational staff training, preparation of school disaster management plans and working on structural safety (UNDP, 2011). The UNDP programme has been part funded by the European Union, the United States Agency for International Development (USAID), the UK Department for International Development (DFID), the Government of Japan and the Australian Agency for International Development. In addition to this, USAID is supporting a Disaster Management Support Project focused on computer modelling and strengthening early warning systems.

Disasters and their Impact on Indian Education

Despite improvements in hazard preparedness, natural hazards continue to inflict a heavy toll on educational provision in India. The 2001 Bhuj earthquake killed 31 teachers and 971 students and damaged 11,761 school buildings, putting 36,584 rooms out of action for holding lessons (NDM, 2006). The two cyclones that hit Orissa in 2009 left more than 10,000 dead, over 7,000 primary schools destroyed and the education of more than two million children severely disrupted (TARU, 2005b). The 2004 tsunami destroyed 360 primary and secondary schools and impacted an estimated 454,000 students along coastal India and in the Andaman and Nicobar islands (UN, 2006). Evaluations of the most recent events – the 6.8 magnitude earthquake that struck the Sikkim/Nepal border on 18 September 2011 and the September 2011 Orissa floods – are provisional. However, in Sikkim it is estimated that 23 school buildings have been completely destroyed while others are being used for emergency shelters (CDRN, 2011). In Orissa, 79 people are reported dead, 5.9 million people affected and damage estimates have already reached $451 million (Indian Express, 2011e). In both states, the school system has virtually closed down, severely disrupting the public examinations for grade 10 students.

The impact of natural disasters goes beyond the tragic loss of life, the disruption of schooling and psychological trauma of survivors. Reconstruction costs can constitute a significant economic drain, with money being spent on maintaining rather than improving the education system. The case of Bihar, one of India's poorest states, is indicative. In 2004, floods destroyed more than

43,000 primary school classrooms and 166 secondary schools. Rebuilding and refurbishment efforts cost an estimated US$ 40 million (UNICEF, 2004).

Education and Disaster Risk Reduction

Providing a comprehensive picture of DRR education in a country as large, dynamic and diverse as India will always be incomplete. However the following tries to provide a snapshot in relation to: higher education and research; school infrastructure; curriculum; school disaster risk reduction; child-based approaches; and targeting (reaching vulnerable children).

Higher Education & Research

India has a rich resource of higher education institutions producing high-level graduates and postgraduates in fields pertinent to DRR such as geophysical studies, and structural engineering. Disaster management, however, requires application of a range of disciplines from structural engineering through to anthropology. In Indian higher education, a total of 17 universities currently offer degree and diploma courses in disaster management (Times of India, 2011). While this appears a healthy total, there is a dearth of data on the number of graduates produced, their employment uptake, or review of the adequacy of the education students receive in the light of the tasks confronted. Moreover, there has been concern expressed that the courses offered are overly focused on structural and management aspects of disaster management to the detriment of the 'soft' socio-anthropological elements (Joshi, 2009).

At postgraduate levels of study, the Jamsetji Tata Centre for Disaster Management (JTCDM), located within the Tata Institute of Social Sciences (TISS), has perhaps an unparalleled record in engagement with disaster management spanning the history of independent India. JTCDM launched its masters programme in disaster management in 2007 with the first modular and multi-disciplinary approach not only within India but across the region (Andharia and Santha, 2007). Its work continues to go beyond the academic, as evidenced by engagement in post-tsunami work in India's Andaman and Nicobar islands (JTCDM, 2008).

School Infrastructure

Children spend a significant proportion of their early lives in schools. It is therefore critical that the structures in which children receive their education are sufficiently resilient to prevailing natural hazards (Schilderman, 1990; OECD, 2004; INEE, 2009; FEMA, 2010; Institute of Structural Engineers, 2010). India has good examples of innovation in school construction that show a particular sensitivity to the influence of buildings on the educational process (Vajpeyi, 2005). It also offers important pointers to approaches in natural hazard resilience (new build and retro-fitting), particularly with regards to earthquakes (Patel et al., undated; Baky, 2003; Holmes et al., 2009) and flooding. As an example, the schools in the riverine areas of Assam have been designed as partially prefabricated structures that can be dismantled and shifted in the event of changes in river course (SSA, undated). In Orissa, DFID financed the construction of over 3,000 new schools following the severe flooding of 1999, including 38 schools that now double up as community cyclone shelters. In rebuilding, careful attention was paid to site location, soil conditions and buildings orientation. Designs have incorporated the use of stilts, plinth protection, roof fixings and ease of community maintenance (TARU, 2004, 2005a; DFID, 2006).

On school building, an interesting contrast is provided by the differing approaches adopted by the decentralised District Primary Education Programme (DPEP) 1994–2002 and its successor, Sarva Shiksha Abhiyan (SSA). DPEP paid particular attention to safety and school building design. As part of the programme, local construction gangs were trained to build to sophisticated designs, using both local and new materials and applying innovative methods (DPEP, 1987, 1988, 1999, 2001). This resulted in well-functioning buildings that have stood the test of time: 'Although a large number of buildings were destroyed or damaged in the devastating earthquake in Gujarat in 2001, not a single building constructed under DPEP suffered any major damage' (SSA, undated, 6).

The mandate of SSA (2003–to date) was to increase rapidly access to primary and elementary education by providing a school within one kilometre of every village. In order to meet this challenge SSA adopted community based implementation:

> Involving the community in planning and construction therefore ensures that the implementation is free from potential environment hazards. Further, by promoting community participation, environmental benefits potentially go beyond the programme, as there are opportunities for building local capacities

> on environmental management, use of appropriate technologies, designs etc. in other similar works.
>
> (SSA, undated: 4)

The approach of SSA, decentralising school-building management to local communities, has had impressive results. Since inception in 2003 the elementary education system in India has grown by close to two-thirds, from 750,000 schools to over 1.30 million schools (DISE, 2010). The Programme has also been praised for its cost effectiveness (NAO, 2010: 32). However, the vast difference in both design and build quality between more complex child-friendly structures of DPEP and the simple 'local builds' of SSA are a striking contrast of the trade-off between quality and mass access.

As Tassios notes, the level of structural resilience of any building involves a social consensus around an acceptable failure probability (Tassios, 2004: 24–5). This acceptable failure probability is in turn a function of the combination of values, income and technological knowledge. In resolving these elements a critical question that emerges is: to what degree is it appropriate to rely on local level community knowledge alone? In the case of SSA, state governments applied their own quality assurance protocols that focused on upholding Indian standard building regulations (SSA, undated: 6). However, standards alone do not guarantee prescribed quality; it is the accuracy with which materials testing and building inspection is carried out that ensures that standards are upheld. With a country the size of India this is clearly going to be variable. Anecdotal evidence suggests that the community-based monitoring of school construction common in Indian school building can be effective (DFID, 2006). However, the degree to which observations stand up against empirical review has yet to be assessed. Communities may provide excellent audit on issues of quantity, quality and price of materials, but the degree to which they can or should be relied upon to provide technical oversight – particularly for more complex buildings – is debatable.

DPEP and SSA have played a major role in India, achieving near universal basic education provision. However, with approximately a third of India's 1.2 billion population below the age of 15, population growth alone will require a continued expansion of school buildings at primary level to maintain this situation. Furthermore, success in primary expansion has predictably driven increasing demand for secondary schooling to which the government responded in 2009 by launching its programme to universalise secondary education (Rastriya Madhyamik Shiksha Abhiyan (RMSA)). In combination, this presents GoI with a daunting challenge in school expansion. In the last 25 years the rapid school expansion seen under DPEP and SSA was enabled in large part by generous community donations of land enabling single-storey school building. The combination of land scarcity and rising food prices has made land an ever more precious commodity in both rural and urban contexts. The possibility of securing new or additional land in India now is therefore often limited. In response, school expansion increasingly involves building the additional storeys (Indian Express, 2011d). This presents significant new challenges for school construction. Without a rigorous inspection regime and meticulous record keeping, it is difficult for engineers to ascertain the capacity of the foundations to bear the extra weight of floors. Indian school planning is thus entering a challenging new phase that will pose serious questions for quality assurance, costing and contingency planning. Of critical significance is the degree to which new builds should be designed with capacity to accommodate additional floors in the future. An approach of this kind will result in higher unit costs initially; but, in the longer term, it will yield significant savings in terms of both finance and human lives.

As detailed above, school expansion to date has involved relatively simple single-storey buildings. A growing trend to build larger multiple-storey buildings raises the critical issue of build standards: quantity and structural surveying, inspection protocols and certification regimes. A recent assessment of global earthquake fatalities provided statistical support for a long-held view that the probability of earthquake-related deaths is 'less a function of geography and more the ability to afford earthquake-resistant construction and to enforce building codes' (Ambraseys and Bilham, 2011). The study points to the combination of poverty restricting the choice of the most appropriate building materials and poor education, which led to substandard construction. Tellingly, the study found that 83% of all deaths caused by the collapse of buildings during earthquakes over the last 30 years occurred in countries considered to be unusually corrupt (Ibid.). While India performed better than predicted by the index created by the authors, the spontaneous collapse of a 15-year-old building, which killed 67 people in Delhi in 2010 (Express India, 2010), poses poignant questions on the extent to which earthquake resilience is compromised by poor/illegal construction in India – an issue recently highlighted by the vice chairman of India's National Disaster Management Agency (Indian Express, 2011a). As Ambraseys and Bilham conclude:

> The structural integrity of a building is no stronger than the social integrity of the builder, and each nation has a responsibility to its citizens to ensure adequate

> inspection. In particular, nations with a history of significant earthquakes and known corruption issues should stand reminded that an unregulated construction industry is a potential killer.
>
> (Ambraseys and Bilham, 2011)

Curriculum

Official recognition of the need to integrate disaster risk management into India's education systems can be traced back to the tenth five-year plan (2002–7). This included a Ministry of Human Resource Development (MHRD) initiative to introduce DRR in state curricula and state examination boards. The areas suggested for inclusion covered included: the nature and types of hazards; natural and man-made disasters and the need for their management; case studies for disaster preparedness and mitigation from different Indian regions; the role of community and schools in disaster management; partnership with various government and non-government agencies; the use of modern and scientific technologies to combat disasters; and survival skills (CBSE, 2004). One of the first boards to act upon the MHRD initiative was the Central Board of Secondary Education (CBSE). It adopted an approach in which disaster preparedness was introduced in grade 8, mitigation in grade 9 and the role of key stakeholders – government, science, community and the individual – in grade 10 (Dey, undated). Though a detailed review of the coverage and nature of disaster preparedness topics in the formal curriculum has yet to be undertaken in India, it does appear that DRR elements have infused the curriculum, particularly in social sciences modules for Grade 8, 9 and 10. Latest estimates indicate that as many as 39 school boards across the country have included disaster management in the curriculum at upper primary school level (Times of India, 2011). This suggests complete national coverage.

A broader regional view of disaster preparedness and the curriculum is provided by the Asia Disaster Preparedness Centre (ADPC, 2007). Drawing from case studies, in India as well as Lao PDR, Pakistan and Sri Lanka, the publication details approaches both where disaster preparedness is integrated across disciplines and where it is detailed as a separate subject. What is clear is that whichever approach is taken the incorporation of disaster risk reduction into the official curriculum is not of itself a guarantee of preparedness for natural disasters. The skill with which the curriculum is 'transacted in the classroom' is critical, as is the degree to which academic earth sciences (which help children understand natural phenomena) are combined with practical skills. The latter need to go beyond the traditional areas of risk assessment and first aid to focus on key survival skills such as the ability to swim and climb. Furthermore, these skills are often strongly gendered and combine with other factors to make women and girls disproportionately vulnerable to disaster events (Swarup et al., 2011; Bray et al., 2008). There is a compelling body of evidence around the particular vulnerability of girls and women to disasters to which the disaster preparedness initiatives have yet to provide an adequate response.

School Disaster Risk Reduction

While individual knowledge and skills are of great importance in DRR they are of themselves insufficient; a fundamental aspect of risk reduction is group behaviour in the face of traumatic events. Thus the degree to which emergency practice drills and contingency plans are embedded within the ethos of a school is particularly important. India's National Disaster School Awareness and Safety Plan Programme (NDM India, 2006) advocates a comprehensive school safety plan fashioned around: prevention mitigation – focusing on reducing or eliminating risk; preparedness – planning for the worst-case scenario; response – definition of appropriate action in the event of a disaster; and recovery – how to provide aftercare and restore education after a crisis. NDM India recommends that such plans incorporate: (i) physical measures: appropriate structural modification, provision of emergency equipment (e.g. fire extinguishers, first aid equipment) and good signage of escape routes; (ii) strong preparatory planning with first response services (including response protocols and sharing of school plans); (iii) the development of building evacuation plans and alarm warnings (appropriate to the nature of the hazard); and (iv) student awareness including hazard searches and regular mock drills. While the logic behind the advice is unquestionable, requests for input into an ongoing study by UNICEF and SEEDS India to document school DRR practice suggest uptake, and particularly the conducting of regular drills, is far from universal.

Child-Based Approaches

In the last decade, growing recognition of the potential of students to act as conduits, taking disaster preparedness beyond the classroom and into the home and community, has led to a growing focus on children as change agents (Antonowicz et al., 2010; DFID/Action AID, 2010; ISDR, 2008; Vanaspongse et al., 2007; Wisner, 2006; Valency, 2007; and Campbell and Yates, 2006). Back et al. capture this as a continuum from expanding knowledge, to enhancing voice, through to taking action (Back et al., 2009). Moreover, Hawrylyshyn has also usefully identified a series of different roles that children can play as change agents along somewhat similar lines (Hawrylyshyn, 2011).

The school-to-community approach of DRR clearly informs much of the documentation around DRR efforts in India. However, detailed analytical scrutiny of both approach and implementation effectiveness remains limited, particularly in comparison to neighbouring Bangladesh. From the information available an EU evaluation report of the GoI–EC-UNDP Disaster Preparedness programme (Cosgrove et al., 2008) details the trade-offs between a 'top-down approach', in which all possible hazards are covered, and a bottom-up approach focused on the risks as identified by the local population, the latter being strongly influenced by the frequency, nature and severity of disaster in recent history. This presents a particular conundrum for infrequent but potentially devastating events such as earthquakes which especially in the less seismically active 'zone three' areas of India may have a return period of several hundred years or more. According to the Cosgrove Report:

> The effectiveness of both the DRM [Disaster Risk Management] and UEVR [Urban Earthquake Vulnerability Reduction] programmes varies with location …. The frequency of hazard events and recent disaster history…. the programme has been far more effective in places where people face frequent disasters such as landslides or flooding than in places which have not experienced major hazards for a generation or more.
>
> (Cosgrove et al., 2008: 5)

The same report also concludes: 'When measured by the holding of mock drills, the national programme has been decreasingly effective as one moves down the hierarchy from the district to the village level' (Ibid.: 5).

Targeting – Reaching Vulnerable Children

Disaster preparedness education does not occur in a vacuum. Schools are rightly regarded as an important medium through which DRR education is both provided and then exported out to the community. However, in taking this view, it is crucial to consider both who is going to school and where they are going. Globally, history consistently shows it is the most disadvantaged groups, forced to live on marginal lands and in substandard housing, who bear the brunt of disasters:

> In the 1998 cyclone in the Indian state of Gujarat, it was the thousands of salt-pan workers living in shanty towns close to their place of work who were most likely to die. Three years later, when an earthquake struck the Bhuj area of Gujarat, deaths were concentrated in the old, dilapidated buildings of the town centre and on the periphery, which housed the rural migrant population.
>
> (Bray et al., 2008: 2)

The children living in such communities are the least likely to be attending school. Access to education for the most marginalized, such as scheduled castes and tribes, is still an ongoing concern in India, particularly at the higher grades (Sedwal and Kamat, 2011). Conversely, in India as elsewhere around the world, there has been a large-scale migration of students from government into low-fee private schools, particularly in urban areas (Strivastava, 2008; French and Kingdon, 2010). The latest National Sample Survey reports 7% of students in private aided and 20% in private unaided schools at primary level, and 12% and 17% respectively at elementary level (NSS, 2009). As the sample survey data do not include private unrecognized schools, it would not be unreasonable to surmise that some 30% of all India's children are being educated outside the government sector. These non-governments schools are less likely to have rigorous safety inspections and generally are the focus of neither government nor NGO/DRR support. If school/community-based approaches to DRR are going to maximize their effectiveness in India, greater consideration of who goes to school and where they go to school is required. As a report from the University of Madras notes: 'The biggest challenge remains in bringing people of different socio-economic backgrounds together, and managing social dynamics and multiple leaders, mainstreaming underprivileged sections and vulnerable categories' (UNESCO, 2007: 32).

Education and Climate Change

The popular paradigm regarding disasters in India as elsewhere places nature as the root cause (Kapoor, 2005, 2010). This can be challenged on two counts. First, it is clear that human determinants – socio-economic status, building quality assurance regimes, and the extent of social safety nets – are strongly associated with the level of human suffering. Secondly, anthromorphic climate change is predicted to increase greatly the number of extreme weather-related climate events such as droughts, floods and cyclones.

Climate projections for India cited in a World Bank paper suggest:

> that India's temperature will rise steadily as greenhouse gases accumulate in the atmosphere. They also predict significant impacts on precipitation, but not consistently, and with different implications for extreme events. A wetter India will experience more floods, while a drier India will experience more droughts.
>
> (Blankespoor et al., 2010: 8)

While the report notes that rising economic development will give India greater resilience, it also notes: 'Since the population is growing, even constant risk (measured as a loss probability) will translate to more losses when it is multiplied by the growing population' (Ibid.: 14). There is a strong likelihood that in the next few decades India will experience more frequent and more severe weather events that will in turn damage education infrastructure and disrupt schooling, impacting upon access and learning attainment. The resultant rehabilitation costs will drain constrained education budgets and require funding to be focused on systems maintenance rather than improvement. For some, climate change will also result in deteriorating household incomes strongly associated with school drop-out, particularly of girls.

While climate change presents new challenges to education, education also provides a powerful means through which to respond. Of the three-pillared response to climate change detailed in the Stern Report, education underpins two, behavioural change and technological development (Stern, 2007). Education has also been shown to play an important role in fertility decline in India (Arokiasamy, et al., 2004). As the UN notes: 'The increase in the education of women and girls contributes to greater empowerment of women, to a postponement of the age of marriage, and to a reduction in the size of families' (UN, 1994).

As the twenty-first century further unfolds, India faces some significant challenges, from climate change and deteriorating agricultural livelihoods to migration and rapid urbanization. The capacity of the country to respond will be in part influenced by the degree to which education equips and empowers the upcoming generations to deal with a rapidly changing world. In a recent speech, India's Minister of Education singled out education as central in determining whether India will realise a demographic dividend or demographic disaster (Denyer, 2011). Ensuring education responds adequately, delivering the much-vaunted demographic dividend will require going beyond education reform that focuses on education access and inputs to addressing India's worryingly low levels of mass educational attainment (Pritchett, 2011; Bhattacharjea et al., 2011). In conjunction, future education planning will need both to factor in the impacts of climate change and to exploit fully the power of education in adaptation and mitigation (Bangay and Bloom, 2010). How this can be approached in the short, medium and long term is illustrated in Figure 3.1.

Conclusion

In India, it is clear that there are committed communities and agencies advocating both disaster risk reduction and environmental education (such as the Centre for Environmental Education). The challenge is that they are working within a system that is producing very low levels of learning. Poor learning outcomes are highly likely to reduce the impact of any behaviour change initiative:

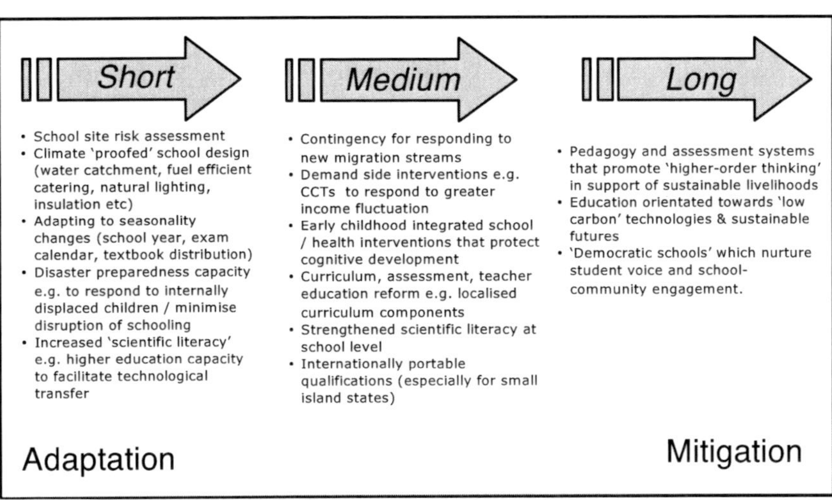

After: Bangay, C. and Blum, N. (2010). Education responses to climate change and quality: two parts of the same agenda? *International Journal of Educational Development* 30, 359–68.

Figure 3.1 Possible Sequence of Educational Responses to Climate Change

> The PISA 2006 assessment of scientific literacy among 15-year-old students offers some important lessons…. Strong performance in science and awareness of global environmental problems tend to go hand in hand, and both are associated with a sense of responsibility supporting sustainable environmental management. Conversely, weak performance in science is associated with lower awareness of environmental problems. Failure in scientific education will mean less widespread – and less informed – public debate on issues such as climate change and wider environmental problems.
>
> (UNESCO, 2009: 37)

If worthwhile Indian DRR and environmental education (EE) initiatives are to retain their relevance, it is critically important that the committed individuals and organisations involved do not lose sight of broader educational issues. As this chapter has highlighted, it is important, for example, to consider: low learning levels; who is going to school and who is not; and where people are going to school. It is especially vital not to neglect the third of children in the non-state sector.

Though it is heartening to see increasing coalescence among the DRR, climate change and EE education communities, there is still a concern that they remain an adjunct to the 'big picture' of improved educational delivery and broader development that education should serve:

> Currently, the communities, strategies and policies related to climate change are disconnected and divergent. Policy has mostly focused on mitigation with country-level GHG emission reductions through international summits and protocols. Other stands of work include adaptation, disaster risk reduction, environmental stewardship, sustainable development, and public awareness and education. However these efforts are rarely coordinated. For instance, since lead responsibility for disaster risk reduction in most governments and non governmental organisations, multilateral institutions and donor agencies rests with units managing emergency response, disaster risk reduction is rarely comprehensively integrated into longer-term development practices. Recent reports have highlighted the confusion created at the country level from this lack of coordination between the wide array of agendas and actors.
>
> (Anderson, 2010)

One of the striking things to emerge in the researching of this chapter is the degree to which the literature, both Indian and international, is dominated by narrative work predominantly focused on documenting perceived best practice in terms of prevention and preparation. While this cannot be considered a systematic assessment, there do appear to be significant gaps in the research literature, particularly empirical research on education and post-disaster recovery and psychology, such as the appropriate age to introduce distressing topics, and the role of education in addressing post-traumatic stress. More strategically, if DRR-EE initiatives are to get the policy attention they deserve, there is an urgent need for more and better cost estimations of losses to education from previous disasters and cost-to-benefit projections around investment in a quality education that equips students to face the future. What little research there is suggests education would pay dividends. 'Educating young women may be one of the best climate change disaster prevention investments in addition to high social rates of return in overall sustainable development goals' (Blankespoor et al., 2010).

Questions for Further Consideration

1. What might be realistic strategies and interventions to propose in order to ensure greater permeation of disaster risk reduction within the non-state sector?
2. This chapter has highlighted the trade-off between education quality and mass access, and implications for disaster risk reduction. What other tensions and trade-offs have similar significance?

Suggestions for Further Reading

This chapter draws on extensive references, detailed below. For further reading:

www.nidp.net is the home page of the official website of India's National Institute of Disaster Management. It is an important conduit for the latest news, documents, publications and networking activity.

www.ndmindia.nic.in is a web portal of the Ministry of Home Affairs dedicated to national disaster management. It too is a rich source of news, information and resources and is constantly updated.

References

Ambraseys, N. and Bilham, R. (2011). Corruption kills. *Nature* 469, 153–5 Available at: www.nature.com/nature/journal/v469/n7329/full/469153a.html [Accessed 6 October 2011].

Anderson, A. (2010). *Combating Climate Change through Quality Education.* Washington, DC: Brookings Institution. Available at: www.preventionweb.net/files/15415_15415brookingspolicybriefclimatecha.pdf [Accessed 17 November 2011].

Andharia, J. and Santha, S. D. (2007). *Curriculum building in disaster management: a process document of evolving a masters' programme at TISS.* JTCDM Working Paper No. 2.

Antonowicz, L., Anderson, A. and Wetheridge, L. (2010). *Child-Centred Disaster Risk Reduction. Building Resilience through Participation: Lessons from Plan International.* London: Plan International. Available at: www.crin.org/docs/CCDRR-Building_resilience_through_participation.pdf [Accessed 6 October 2011].

Arokiasamy, P., McNay, K. and Cassen, R. H. (2004). Female education and fertility decline: recent developments in the relationship. *Economic and Political Weekly,* 39, 41, 4503–7.

Asian Disaster Preparedness Center (ADPC) (2007). *Integrating Disaster Risk Reduction into School Curriculum: Mainstreaming Disaster Risk Reduction into Education. Regional Consultative Committee on Disaster Management.* Bangkok: Asian Disaster Preparedness Center. Available at: www.ineesite.org/assets/ADPCIntegratingDRRIntoSchoolCurriculum.pdf [Accessed 24 June 2011].

Back, E., Cameron, C. and Tanner, T. (2009). *Children and Disaster Risk Reduction: Taking Stock and Moving Forward.* Geneva: UNICEF. Available at: www.unicef.org.uk/Documents/Publications/drr-takingstock.pdf [Accessed 8 October 2011].

Baky, L. (2003). A report concerning the Maharashtra earthquake: a grassroots re-building guide, in *Disaster Relief – Support for Aid Agencies (Disk 1)* London: Institute of Structural Engineers.

Bangay, C. and Blum, N. (2010). Education responses to climate change and quality: two parts of the same agenda? *International Journal of Educational Development* 30, 359–68.

Bhattacharjea, S., Wadhwa, W. and Banerji, R. (2011). *Inside Primary Schools: A Study of Teaching and Learning in Rural India.* New Delhi: ASER. Available at: images2.asercentre.org/homepage/Teaching-learning_study.pdf [Accessed 08 November 2011].

Blankespoor, B., Dasgupta, S., Laplante, B. and Wheeler, D. (2010). *Adaption to Climate Extremes in Developing Countries: The Role of Education.* Washington D.C: World Bank. Policy Research Working Paper 5342.

Bray, I., Chughtai, S., Kenny, S., Narayan, S., Phillips, B. and Soni, M. (2008). *Rethinking Disasters: Why Death and Destruction is Not Nature's Fault But Human Failure.* New Delhi: Oxfam. Available at: www.preventionweb.net/files/1764_oxfamindiarethinkingdisasters.pdf [Accessed 17 November 2011].

Campbell, J. and Yates, R. (2006). *Lessons for Life: Building a Culture of Safety and Resilience to Disasters Through Schools: A Briefing Paper.* Bangalore: Action Aid. Available at: www.unisdr.org/eng/public_aware/world_camp/2006-2007/iddr/docs/UK-actionaid-report.pdf [Accessed 6 October 2011].

Central Board of Secondary Education (CBSE) (2004). *Towards a Safer India: Education in Disaster Management.* New Delhi: Central Board of Secondary Education. Available at: www.ndmindia.nic.in/WCDRDOCS/Towards%20A%20Safer%20India-CBSE.pdf [Accessed 06 October 2011].

Columbia University (2005). India Natural Disaster Profile. Web page: www.ldeo.columbia.edu/chrr/research/profiles/india.html [Accessed 17 November 2011].

Corporate Disaster Resource Network (CDRN) (2011). *Sikkim Earthquake 18ᵗʰ September 2011 Situation Report*. Online: Corporate Disaster Resource Network. Available at: cdrn.org.in/blog/wp-content/uploads/2011/09/Himalayan-Sikkim-Earthquake-Situation-Report-2011CDRN.pdf [Accessed 17 November 2011].

Cosgrove, J., Bhatt, M., Silver, M. and Alexander, P. (2008). *GoI-EC-UNDP Disaster Preparedness in India – Evaluation Report*. New Delhi: European Commission.

Denyer, S. (2011). Amid population boom, India hopes for 'demographic dividend' but fears disaster. *Washington Post* 16 October. Available at: www.washingtonpost.com/world/asia_pacific/amid-population-boom-india-hopes-for-demographic-dividend-but-fears-disaster/2011/10/12/gIQA9I4nmL_print.html [Accessed 8 November 2011].

Department for International Development (DFID) (2006). *Department for International Development (UK) Project Completion Report of the Orissa Post Cyclone Reconstruction of Primary Schools*. London/New Delhi: DFID.

Dey, B. (undated). *Disaster Management in Education and Training of Teachers and Students: Catch Them Young*. Online publication. Available at: ndmindia.nic.in/Workshop_ppt/School_Safety/BalakaDey_files/frame.htm [Accessed 24 June 2011].

DFID and Action Aid (2010). *Good Practices and Lessons Learned: Disaster Risk Reduction through Schools*. Kathmandu: Action Aid and DFID. Available at: www.preventionweb.net/files/18705_186 96actionaiddrrgoodpracticesbook1.pdf [Accessed 6 October 2011].

District Information System for Education (DISE) (2010). *Flash Statistics, DISE 2009–10*. Online. Available at: www.dise.in/ [Accessed 2 October 2011].

District Primary Education Programme (DPEP) (1987). *Lets Work Together – A Community Construction Manual*. New Delhi: DPEP.

DPEP (1988). *A Guide to Design for Better Learning Environment*. New Delhi: DPEP.

—(1999). *Building Rural Primary Schools – Towards Improved Designs*. New Delhi: DPEP.

—(2001). *Child Friendly Elements for Rural Primary Schools – An Engineer's Handbook*. New Delhi: DPEP.

Emergency Events Database (EM-DAT) (2011). Online. Available at: www.emdat.be/ [Accessed 6 October 2011].

Express India (2010). Delhi building collapse: 67 dead as survivors stare at bleak future. 16 November. *Express India*. Online. Available at: www.expressindia.com/latest-news/Delhi-building-collapse-67-dead-as-survivors-stare-at-bleak-future/711961/ [Accessed 6 October 2011].

Federal Emergency Management Agency (FEMA) (2010). *Design Guide for School Safety Against Earthquakes, Floods, and High Winds*. Washington DC: US Department of Homeland Security. Available at: www.fema.gov/library/viewRecord.do?id=1986 [Accessed 2 October 2011].

French, R. and Kingdon, G. (2010). *The Relative Effectiveness of Private and Government Schools in Rural India: Evidence from Aser Data*, DoQSS Working Paper No. 10–03. London: Institute of Education. Available at: repec.ioe.ac.uk/REPEc/pdf/qsswp1003.pdf [Accessed 10 October 2011].

Government of India (GoI) (2005). *Disaster Management Act 2005* Available at: ndma.gov.in/ndma/pdf/DM_Act2005.pdf [Accessed 26 August 2011].

—(2009). *National Policy on Disaster Management.* New Delhi: National Disaster Management Authority, Government of India, Ministry Of Home Affairs. Available at: nidm.Gov.In/Pdf/Policies/Ndm_Policy2009.Pdf [Accessed 26 June 2011].

—(2011a). *State Level Programmes for the Strengthening of Disaster Management in India. Initiatives by the Ministry of Home Affairs.* New Delhi: GoI.

—(2011b). *The National Census.* Available at: censusindia.gov.in/ [Accessed 23 September 2011].

Hawrylyshyn, K. (2011). *Sharing Plan's Experiences on Education, Climate and Environmental Change.* Presentation given at the UKFIET Conference, September 2011.

Holmes, W. T., Rodgers, J. E., Wij, S., Kumar, H., Tobin, L. T. and Seth, A. (2009). Seismic risk reduction for schools with stone slab roof systems in Delhi. *Proceedings of the 2009 ATC and SEI Conference on Improving the Seismic Performance of Existing Buildings and Other Structures,* 258–67.

Indian Express (2010). 38 Indian cities fall in moderate to high risk seismic zones. *Indian Express* 10 April. Available at: www.indianexpress.com/news/38-indian-cities-fall-in-moderate-to-high-risk-seismic-zones/774197 [Accessed 1 October 2011].

—(2011a). Building norms compliance poor in state, says NDMA vice-chairman. *Indian Express* 3 July. Available at: www.indianexpress.com/news/building-norms-compliance-poor-in-state-says-ndma-vicechairman/811985 [Accessed 6 October 2011].

—(2011b). India carries out tsunami warning system test. *Indian Express* 13 October. Available at: www.indianexpress.com/news/india-carries-out-tsunami-warning-system-test/859283 [Accessed 17 November 2011].

—(2011c). India second in world for natural disasters: UN. *Indian Express* 24 January. Available at: www.indianexpress.com/news/india-ranks-second-in-world-for-natural-disa/741701/ [Accessed 18 November 2011].

—(2011d). Many school buildings in walled city are over 50. *Indian Express* 29 September. Available at: www.indianexpress.com/news/many-schools-buildings-in-walled-city-are-over-50/853405 [Accessed 17 November 2011].

—(2011e). Water gushed in from two states, the tide too turned against Orissa. *Indian Express* 29 September. Available at: www.indianexpress.com/news/water-gushed-in-from-two-states-the-tide-too-turned-against-orissa/853241 [Accessed 17 November 2011].

Institute of Structural Engineers (2010). *Disaster Relief – Support for Aid Agencies (Disk 1)* Two CD compendium. London: Institute of Structural Engineers.

Inter-Agency Network for Education in Emergencies (INEE) (2009). *Safer School Construction Initiative: Guidance Notes on Safer School Construction.* No Place: ISDR, INEE and World Bank. Available at: www.ineesite.org/index.php/post/safer_school_construction_initiative [Accessed 2 October 2011].

International Strategy for Disaster Reduction (ISDR) (2008). *Safe Schools in Safe Territories: Reflections on the Role of the Educational Community in Risk Management.* Geneva: Central American Educational and Cultural Coordinator, United Nations Children's Fund & the International Strategy for Disaster Reduction. Available at: www.ineesite.org/uploads/documents/store/Safe%20Schools%20in%20Safe%20Territories.pdf [Accessed 6 October 2011].

Jamsetji Tata Centre for Disaster Management (JTCDM) (2008). *Towards Sustainable Development of the Andaman and Nicobar Islands: A Three Year Post Tsunami Engagement (2004-2007)*. Mumbai: JTCDM.

Joshi, P. C. (2009). *The Status of Disaster-Related Courses in Indian Universities*. Online: nidm.gov.in/idmc2/session_education.asp [Accessed 1 October 2011].

Kapoor, A. (2005). Insensitive India: attitudes towards disaster prevention and management. *Economics and Political Weekly* 40, 42.

—(2010). *Vulnerable India: A Geographical Study of Disasters*. New Delhi: Sage.

Kostman, C. J. D. (1996). The demise of utopia: contexts of civilizational collapse in the Bronze Age Indus Valley. *Journal of the Association of Graduates in Near Eastern Studies* 6 (2). Available at: www.adventurecorps.com/archaeo/collapse.html [Accessed 3 September 2011].

Maplecroft (2010). *Big Economies of the Future – Bangladesh, India, Philippines, Vietnam and Pakistan – Most at Risk from Climate change*. Online. Available at: maplecroft.com/about/news/ccvi.html [Accessed 26 August 2011].

National Audit Office (NAO) (2010). *DFID: Bilateral Support to Primary Education*. London: NAO.

National Disaster Management (NDM) (2006). *School Awareness and Safety Programme: A Step Towards School Safety*. Online. Available at: www.ndmindia.nic.in/Workshop_ppt/School_Safety/SASP%20061104_files/frame.htm [Accessed 3 September 2011].

National Sample Survey Office (NSS) (2009). *Education in India 2007-08 Participation and Expenditure – Highlights*. New Delhi: GoI. Available at: mospi.nic.in/Mospi_New/upload/nsso/532_highlights.pdf [Accessed 20 June 2011].

New Scientist (2010). Climate changes most vulnerable list. *New Scientist*, October. Available at: www.newscientist.com/article/mg20827832.400-asia-tops-climate-changes-most-vulnerable-list.html [Accessed 26 August 2011].

OECD (2004). *Educational Facilities and Risk Management – Natural Disasters*. London: OECD. Available at: www.oecdbookshop.org/oecd/get-it.asp?REF=9504011e.pdf&TYPE=browse [Accessed 18 November 2011].

Patel, D., Pindoria, K. and Hughes, R. (undated). A guide for repair, strengthening and new build of low-rise domestic buildings damaged by the 26 January 2001 earthquake in Gujarat, India, in *Disaster Relief –Support for Aid Agencies (Disk 1)* (2010) London: Institute of Structural Engineers.

Pritchett, L. (2011). *Interview with Lant Pritchett: People Can't Believe the Same Economy that Produces 100,000 Students a Year in Global Top 10% Also Churns out Millions With Zero Skills*. Online. Available at: www.indianexpress.com/news/people-cant-believe-the-same-economy-that-produces-100-000-students-a-year-in-global-top-10-also-churns-out-millions-with-zero-skills/872364/ [Accessed 09 November 2011].

Sarva Shiksha Abhiyan (SSA) (Undated). Sarva Shiksha Abhiyan: *An Environmental Assessment*. New Delhi: Educational Consultants India Ltd. Available at: www.education.nic.in/ssa/environment-ssa-pt1.pdf [Accessed 2 October 2011].

Schilderman, T. (1990). Earthquake protection for poor people's houses. *Appropriate Technology Magazine* Volume 17/1, in *Disaster Relief – Support for Aid Agencies (Disk 1) (2010)*. London: Institute of Structural Engineers.

Sedwal, M. and Kamat, S. (2011). Education and social equity in elementary education, in Govinda, R. (ed.) *Who Goes to School. Exploring Exclusion in Indian Education.* New Delhi: Oxford University Press.

Srivastava, P. (2008). The shadow institutional framework: towards a new institutional understanding of an emerging private school sector in India. *Research Papers in Education* 23, 4, December, 451–75.

Stern, N. (2007). *The Economics of Climate Change: The Stern Review.* Cambridge: Cambridge University Press. Available at: www.hm-treasury.gov.uk/sternreview_index.htm [Accessed 18 November 2011].

Structural Engineers (UK) (2010). *Two CD Compendium.*

Swarup, A., Dankelman, I., Ahluwalia, K. and Hawrylyshyn, K. (ed. Goulds, S.) (2011). *Weathering the Storm: Adolescent Girls and Climate Change.* Available at: plan-international.org/files/global/publications/emergencies/weathering-storm.pdf [Accessed 18 November 2011].

TARU (2004 & 2005a). *Orissa Post Cyclone School Reconstruction Project: Inception Report (2004), Phase 1 Report (2004), Phase 2 Report (2004), Phase 3 Report (2005), Report on Progress (2005)* New Delhi: TARU.

—(2005b). *Joint Monitoring Review of Orissa Post-Cyclone Reconstruction of Primary Schools Project.* New Delhi: TARU.

The Energy and Resources Institute (TERI) (2010). *Climate Resilient and Sustainable Urban Development.* New Delhi: TERI. Available at: preventionweb.net/go/18315 [Accessed 18 November 2011].

Times of India (2011). India still long way from disaster mitigation. *Times of India* 30 April. Available at: articles.timesofindia.indiatimes.com/2011-04-30/varanasi/29490574_1_disaster-management-disaster-mitigation-diploma [Accessed 1 October 2011].

United Nations (UN) (1994). *Ch. XI, Para. 11.3 International Conference on Population and Development – Cairo.* Online. Available at: www.un.org/popin/icpd2.htm [Accessed 18 November 2011].

—(1999). *The World at Six Billion United Nations.* Online. Available at: www.un.org/esa/population/publications/sixbillion/sixbilpart1.pdf [Accessed 23 September 2011].

—(2006). *Tsunami: India Two Years After: A Joint Report of the United Nations, World Bank, and Asian Development Bank.* No Place: UN, World Bank and ADB. Available at: www.adb.org/Documents/Reports/Tsunami-India/tsunami-india.pdf [Accessed 18 November 2011].

United Nations Children's Fund (UNICEF) (2004). *Schooling Spluttering to a Start in Flood-Affected Districts of Bihar.* Online. Available at: www.unicef.org/infobycountry/india_23443.html [Accessed 29 September 2011].

United Nations Development Programme (UNDP) (2010). *School Children Teach Disaster Response – International Day for Disaster Risk Reduction.* Online. Available at: www.undp.org.in/School_children_teach_disaster_response [Accessed 3 September 2011].

—(2011). *School Safety Initiatives – GoI-UNDP Disaster Risk Management Programme.* New Delhi: UNDP/GoI.

United Nations Education, Scientific and Cultural Organisation (UNESCO) (2007). Madras University: India Report, in *Natural Disaster Preparedness and Education for Sustainable Development.* Bangkok: UNESCO.

—(2009). *EFA Global Monitoring Report 2009: Overcoming Inequality: Why governance Matters.* Oxford: Oxford University Press and UNDP. Available at: unesdoc.unesco.org/images/0017/001776/177683e.pdf [Accessed 18 November 2011].

Valency, R. A. (ed.) (2007). *Towards a Culture of Prevention: Disaster Risk Reduction Begins at School: Good Practices and Lessons Learned.* Geneva: UNISDR. Available at: www.ineesite.org/uploads/documents/store/doc_1_DRRBeginsSchool.pdf [Accessed 6 October 2011].

Vajpeyi, K. (2005). *Building as Learning Aid.* New Delhi: Vinyas, Centre for Architectural Research and Design.

Vanaspongse, C., Ratanachena, S., Rattanapan, J., Chutong, S. and Intraraksa, R. (2007). *Training Manual: Child-Led Disaster Risk Reduction in Schools and Communities.* Bangkok: Save the Children Sweden – Southeast Asia and The Pacific Regional Office. Available at: seap.savethe-children.se/Global/scs/SEAP/publication/publication%20pdf/Disaster/DRR%20training%20manual%20_eng.pdf [Accessed 6 October 2011].

Wisner, B. (2006). *Let our Children Teach Us! A Review of the Role of Education and Knowledge in Risk Reduction.* Bangalore: Books for Change/UNISDR. Available at: www.unisdr.org/eng/task%20force/working%20groups/knowledge-education/docs/Let-our-Children-Teach-Us.pdf [Accessed 6 October 2011].

4 Hurricane Katrina in the United States: Make Levees, Not War

Benjamin Newton

Chapter Outline

Introduction

At around 6 a.m. on Monday 29 August 2005, Hurricane Katrina struck the Southern Coast of Louisiana. While this region is historically familiar with the strong storms that emerge from the warm summer waters of the Atlantic Ocean and Gulf of Mexico, Hurricane Katrina took only one day to leave its mark as one of the worst environmental disasters in United States history. For those who have followed the storm's build-up and aftermath, the city of New

Orleans has become the poster child for the toll paid. By Tuesday 30 August, 80% of the city flooded, leaving approximately 50,000 to 100,000 people stranded within the municipality's borders (Brookings Institution, 2005: 3). The impact and reaction directed towards the city's poor and immobile, in particular, has left many to question the capabilities and priorities of the world's strongest economic and military superpower.

Even as the floodwaters have receded, the devastation wreaked along the Gulf States of Louisiana, Mississippi, Alabama and Florida still impacts the vast infrastructures of these locales today. The price tag of rebuilding remains immense. For instance, the Army Corps of Engineers has estimated that the cost to repair the coastline and expansive levee system alone will hover between $70 billion and $125 billion (Schleifstein, 2009, 1). When related to the estimated $118 billion that the United States will spend on the wars in Afghanistan and Iraq in the 2012 fiscal year, it is clear why some local residents of the Big Easy sport the T-shirt with the message 'Make Levees, Not War'.

In relation to the effect and aftermath of the Hurricane, New Orleans' education system serves as an interesting case study for how one can examine the connection between natural disasters and education. On one level, it illustrates how schools cannot escape the environments in which they operate. On another level the circumstances reveal how human actions can heighten the negative consequences of emergencies. Yet, when discussing progress specific to New Orleans, it is important to remember that context matters. In the words of the British educational comparativist, Michael Sadler, in 1900 (Sadler, in Higginson, 1979: 49): a system of education is a 'living thing, the outcome of forgotten struggles'. While our understanding of the effect of Hurricane Katrina on New Orleans' schools can be placed within the setting of the impact of floods on education globally, decisions made since the storm must be understood as a result of the events that occurred.

This chapter will discuss both the immediate and long-term impact of Hurricane Katrina on the education system of New Orleans. First, what follows will place the case within the context of how natural disasters, in particular flooding, have an impact on schools globally. Second, the investigation will shed light on why New Orleans is both susceptible to flooding and how the city's demographics contributed to the humanitarian crisis. Finally, the chapter will review the New Orleans case in greater detail. This will include a discussion of how the system responded immediately and has adapted over time. Specifically, the chapter will evaluate the state of Louisiana's effort to embrace the Charter

School movement. Echoing the sentiments of some educational comparativists, such as Sadler and Bereday (1964), this chapter will posit that while scholars and practitioners can glean positive lessons from studying the case, they should also exercise caution in applying those lessons to other circumstances.

Background on the Global Relationship between Natural Disasters, Flooding and Education

With their dependence on human capital, schools cannot operate separately from the environments in which they function. Unsurprisingly, conflict and poverty surround schools with low community engagement and student performance. When thinking of the types of emergency scenarios that schools encounter globally, the kinds of disasters can vary extensively. As reflected in the work of Heneveld and Craig (1996), there are many inputs that determine the viability of a particular school unit. Popular conflict and flooding can have both similar and disparate consequences depending on a number of factors.

The question of why the protection of education, schools and children matters is an important one, but often goes ignored in the face of large-scale devastation. When emergency situations first occur, those responsible for reacting have some clear primary priorities. Sommers (1999) offers a succinct general description in his work studying refugee crises:

> For humanitarian officials, there's food and plastic sheeting to distribute, water to sanitize, and emergency medical services to set up. Assessments must be made, funding sought and transport arranged. A system of coordination is devised. Protection concerns have to be worked out with local government officials. Soon, tasks like registering refugees or internally displaced persons, handing out donated clothes and blankets, and taking precautions against epidemics are carried out. For all officials involved, time is at a premium and issues of management and logistics dominate.
>
> (Sommers, 1999: 2)

The primary concern for first-responders is the protection of human life and taking care of those who are without the most basic of necessities. It is under these circumstances that the effect on education will vary. 'Conflicts and emergencies... can have wide-ranging impacts on education, from disruption of regular school schedules and destruction of learning materials and schools to the displacement and death of students, teachers and parents' (Winthrop et al., 2010: 2). Those affected can range from large portions of the population to individuals, therefore complicating the determination of an appropriate response.

As a partial aside, when thinking about the criticism of US spending in regard to the relationship between rebuilding New Orleans and military expenditures, the arguments are not black and white. The United States spends 4.7% of Gross Domestic Product (GDP) on its military. This is a relatively high figure. By way of further national example, earthquake-prone Turkey and flood-prone Bangladesh allocate 2.7% and 1.0% respectively (SIPRI, 2011). The figures for spending on education in the abovementioned countries, as a percentage of GDP, are as follows: USA 5.5%; Turkey, 2.9%; and Bangladesh 2.2% (UNESCO, 2010). It should also be added, however, that, when disasters strike, it is often the military that takes a lead role in rescue and recovery operations, so a level of capacity of this kind is often vital. As will be returned to below, the US military did indeed play a significant role following Hurricane Katrina.

When normal school schedules and activities do resume (assuming that such structures provided safe and secure environments in the first place), adults can mitigate the harm done to children. However, 'Children living in countries affected by emergencies are less likely to enrol continually, participate and complete basic schooling' (Winthrop et al., 2010: 2). When the disruption is prolonged, suffering can last a lifetime. As Shriver writes, 'Children's needs are unique, especially when prescribing… physical and mental health interventions and purchasing equipment and supplies' (Shriver, 2009: xiii). The ability to administer meaningful mental health services is extremely difficult as it often relies on a minority of highly qualified individuals. In New Orleans, while much of the education infrastructure is well into the rebuilding process, little is known of the mental health of returning students subsequent to the floods. Accordingly, the degree to which an education system can 'bounce back' is extremely relevant to supporting children. At the most basic level, without education, one's ability to protect oneself is weakened, potentially perpetuating a cycle of despair.

A related point, and one discussed in Chapter 1 and elsewhere within this volume, is that when disasters strike, it is the least developed regions and the most vulnerable and weaker sections of society that tend to suffer the most. While the United States is one of the most advanced countries on earth, there are huge in-country disparities. As this chapter will go on to explain, New Orleans is one of the most challenged cities in the country, as measured by many social indicators, especially educational – and this is important for understanding both impact and response.

Two basic perspectives support the benefits of maintaining some semblance of an education system during disasters. First, in the immediate aftermath of a disaster or emergency:

> Education and its practitioners can provide a safe place for children, meet the psychological needs of children, offer daily structure, facilitate the screening of children for specific protection needs, enhance children's understanding of what they've lived through, convey survival messages and sometimes promote reconciliation.
>
> (Sommers, 2003: 16)

Second, the existence of an educated population will ultimately make the rebuilding process easier – an especially important point to consider in view of the caveat about New Orleans itself, noted above. More simply put, an individual's ability to read and access basic information can go a long way, especially in the absence of coordinated emergency services.

In further identifying how best to protect children, preparation can be difficult, particularly when the most vulnerable fail to anticipate or understand properly the disaster scenarios. Nothing better exemplifies this point than the cases surrounding natural disasters. Human history, evolution and advancement have incorporated a better understanding of how the environment works. The ability of populations to spread has directly involved a control over nature. Yet, as has been observed by victims, refugees and onlookers in many cases, humans' perceived command over the environment is often fleeting.

Perhaps lying at the centre of concern for the future is human comprehension of climate change. Whether or not one subscribes to theories of man-made global warming, recent climate change globally has resulted in phenomena that have had a direct effect on the Earth's naturally occurring climate cycles, as they are presently understood. The National Aeronautics and Space Administration (NASA) states that the Earth's average temperature has steadily climbed since the 1970s (Lawshe, 2010). Moreover, the warmest ten years recorded have occurred in the last twelve years. The International Panel on Climate Change (IPCC) further cites that the increasing presence of carbon dioxide (CO2) in the Earth's atmosphere has led to the rising of both the depth and warmth of the world's major waterways. Increasing temperatures and sea levels in particular have had an impact on the occurrences of floods globally. These are all considerations that make New Orleans itself ever more vulnerable.

Episodes of flooding are obviously not modern events. They are a natural part of the environmental cycle. The evolution of human history includes innovations that have increased the capacity to control water. While the earliest populations dealt with flooding as a direct result of needing to live in fertile regions (Kersting, 2010), today, through advanced engineering, the construction of dams and other reinforcements has allowed humans not only to prevent flooding but also to access previously uninhabitable areas. The city of New Orleans, located on the Mississippi delta, was originally founded on naturally occurring areas of high ground, known as 'levees'. However, significant areas of the modern city and its surroundings encompass land that was formerly swamp and marshland – occupation made possible by the building of artificial levees and other forms of flood defence.

Similar to other natural disasters, flooding can shut down an entire education system. Water has the power to destroy and displace. Flooding can wash away years of work and development in a matter of moments. No clearer examples exist than with the flooding caused by the recent Indian Ocean (2004) and Japanese (2011) tsunamis. With respect to the former, 200,000 people in 14 countries were killed in minutes and the struggle to recover fully will take decades. Recent significant floods in the United Kingdom (2007), China (2010) and Pakistan (2011) have similarly displaced thousands of people and caused billions of dollars in damage. In Bangladesh, annual flooding is causing significant changes to the country's geographical borders. 'The United Nations estimates that by the end of the century, 18% of the country will disappear, leaving 30 million people displaced' (Rivers, 2010).

Among countries within the Organization for Economic Cooperation and Development (OECD), floods are the most damaging of all potential environmental disasters (OECD, 2006a: 7). Within Europe between 1980 and 2002:

> Flood disasters represent half of the fatalities and a third of economic losses due to natural disasters in the world. In the European Union … the greatest number of floods occurred in France (22 per cent of EU total), Italy (17 per cent) and the UK (12 per cent). The highest number of fatalities occurred in Italy (38 per cent), followed by Spain (20 per cent) and France (17 per cent). The greatest economic

> losses occurred in Germany and Italy (both €11 billion), followed by Spain and
> the UK (both around €6 billion). In the last decade, the EU has launched around
> 50 research projects in this field, with a total budget of €58 million, in areas such
> as flood risk assessment, flood hazard and risk mapping, flood forecasting and
> preventative land-use planning.
>
> (OECD, 2006b: 16)

If floods are natural realities, how do governments and people prepare? Generally speaking, a variety of geographic, economic, physical and cultural characteristics determine locations at greatest risk (OECD, 2006c: 22). Of these, cultural vulnerability is perhaps the most troubling because it reflects the ability of a population to recognize the threats against it (ibid.). As will be examined with the New Orleans case below, the demographic composition of a population can severely exacerbate the potential for loss.

In literature discussing the relationship between education and flooding, it is macro level considerations that predominate. Yet it is the local level where those who wish to understand the relationship between education and flooding can gain greater information and perspective. The experiences of individual schools and teachers can tell us a tremendous amount about what reactions work best and why. There are lessons to be learned from both immediate and long-term responses. In Bangladesh, for instance, there has been a rise in the number of 'floating' schools (Rivers, 2010). In the case of Hurricane Katrina, the response to the absolute destruction of a school system's physical and human infrastructure provides a view into what it means to 'start over'.

The Geographic and Demographic Vulnerability of New Orleans

When the citizens of New Orleans prepared for Hurricane Katrina, it was an exercise they had participated in many times. The geographic location of the city makes flooding and hurricanes environmental inevitabilities for its inhabitants. With parts of the city below sea level and located between two major bodies of water in Lake Pontchartrain (North) and the Mississippi River (South), residents of the 'Big Easy' have long been aware of the potential for flooding, in particular. The last major flooding of the city, however, was a distant memory for many as it occurred after 1964's 'Hurricane Betsy'. Yet, with many passing years since Hurricane Betsy, the effect of 'false alarms' on the population undoubtedly affected the seriousness with which the city prepared for potential future storms.

Over the last century, New Orleans has become significantly more vulnerable to the storms that emerge from the Gulf of Mexico. Louisiana's Gulf Coast consists of hundreds of square miles of wetlands that have functioned as a natural buffer. These storms, which feed off warm water, slow down when they hit land. Since 1930, an estimated 1900 square miles of wetlands have eroded (National Geographic Society, 2010). Historically the wetlands have been sustained by fresh water and silt, brought by the natural flooding of the Mississippi River (Time, 2010). Humans have contributed directly to the wetland's destruction. First, the construction of levees to prevent flooding has kept essential resources from reaching the wetlands. As a result, salt water from the Gulf of Mexico has been able to infiltrate the ecosystem and destroy freshwater plants. As the plants die, the wetlands dry up and sink under eroding salt water from the Gulf. Second, the removal of drinking water has further accelerated this loss. Louisiana is literally sinking into the sea. As a result, the natural shield of New Orleans has weakened. There are thus many implications for the role that education can play in environmental awareness and response. However, it is beyond the scope of this chapter to explore these considerations here.

In addition to New Orleans' geographic vulnerability, the city's demographic composition also contributed to an inability to prepare and respond to the crisis. In fact, Mississippi, Alabama and Louisiana represent three of the poorest states in the United States. The median income of the population of each of these three states was in the bottom 10% at the time of Hurricane Katrina (Sherman and Shapiro, 2005: 1). It is estimated, for instance, that nearly 1 million of the 5.8 million affected by Hurricane Katrina lived in poverty (ibid.: 2). Moreover, according to statistics from the year 2000, 54% of New Orleans residents did not own a car, van or truck (ibid.: 2). When Ray Nagin, then the mayor of New Orleans, called for the mandatory evacuation of the city on Sunday 28 August, at 11:00 a.m., many individuals were not able to leave through their own means because of lack of mobility. After the city flooded, approximately '62,000 water, roof and attic rescues by either boat or helicopter' became necessary in the subsequent five days (Jonkman et al., 2009: 679).

Where sometimes the effects of natural disasters cannot be anticipated by those affected, much of the legacy of Hurricane Katrina involves a discussion of how human actions could have lessened the loss of life and infrastructure. While, in 1965, 40 people died from Hurricane Betsy (ibid.: 678), 1,400 perished from Katrina. Furthermore, of the 853 bodies available for study, 'nearly 85% were older than 51, 60% older than 65 and almost half were older than 75 years of age' (Schleifstein, 2009). Of those deaths, 516 (67%) were caused by a presumed direct exposure to flood waters (Jonkman, 2009, 686). In other words, this was a population already known to be at risk.

A General Perspective on the Impact of Hurricane Katrina on Education

Prior to Hurricane Katrina, New Orleans possessed one of the lowest-performing education systems in the United States. The condition of the system has led many to question whether it exacerbated both the poor preparation and disastrous response. Correlating with the poverty of the region, the Gulf States traditionally rank among the poorest on state standardized assessments. In New Orleans, prior to Hurricane Katrina, 'two thirds of the region's public schools were deemed academically unacceptable ... half the public school students didn't graduate from high school, and .... Forty per cent of adults living in the city of New Orleans were illiterate' (Greater New Orleans, 2010). By the end of the 2005 academic year, 70% and 49% of students in the eighth grade scored below 'basic' level in Mathematics and English Language Arts respectively (Louisiana Department of Education, 2005). While researchers can link educational performance to poverty and poverty to mobility (or lack thereof), one can only theorize about the impact of the population's basic numeracy and literacy skills on preparation and response.

The impact of Hurricane Katrina on New Orleans' education infrastructure was devastating. This reality was reflected across a number of essential public services that were utterly incapacitated. In 2006, the Government Accountability Office (GAO) reported on the devastation regionally:

> Hurricane Katrina exposed difficulties in continuing essential government operations, particularly at the local level. In the devastated areas, local government infrastructure was destroyed and essential government employees, including many first responders, were evacuated or victimized by the storms. Local officials

> in Mississippi and Louisiana told us of cases where there was limited continuity of operations for public safety and service agencies because both structures and equipment were destroyed or too damaged to use. For example, one Mississippi County lost all its public buildings located south of Interstate 10. We were also told criminal justice facilities in New Orleans and St Bernard parishes were disabled as both jurisdictions had to evacuate jails damaged by flood waters.
>
> (Fagnoni, 2006: 16)

Not only was there was an immediate disabling of basic public services by the storm, it has taken time for some of those to return. According to available data, six months after the storm a mere 40% of hospitals and 15% of schools were open. One whole year after the event, the figure was still only 50% and 19% respectively (Liu, 2006: 7).

Aside from official reports and statistics, personal accounts of those who remained in the city paint a vivid picture of the lack of structure and personnel organization that existed in general. For instance, Eggers (2009), detailing the experiences of Abdulraham Zeitoun, a Syrian-born New Orleans resident, provides a sense of the lawlessness that had descended upon the city. When reaching an area in the Uptown portion of the city near Carrollton Street, Zeitoun:

> expected that there might be people on Carrollton … it seemed a logical thoroughfare for rescue and military boats – but when he got close, he saw no official personnel at all. Instead he saw a group of men gathered at the Shell station just across the street …. The men, about eight or nine of them, were carrying full garbage bags from the station's office and loading them into a boat. It was the first looting he had seen since the storm …. This was an organized group of criminal opportunists who were not simply taking what they needed to survive. They were stealing money and goods from the gas station, and they were operating in numbers that seemed designed to intimidate anyone, like Zeitoun, who might see them or try to impede them.
>
> (Eggers, 2009: 128–9)

The local education system could not escape these kinds of reality in the aftermath.

Of particular significance was the degree of population displacement. Along the Gulf Coast, 750,000 families were forced by Hurricane Katrina and subsequent flooding to leave their homes (Katz, 2006a: 1). Within Louisiana and Mississippi, 700 schools were damaged or destroyed and 370,000 students were forced to move (Pastorek, 2009: 1). These figures do not disaggregate the numbers and types of school practitioners who were involved in this mass exodus of the region. Certainly, Louisiana's education system took a huge brunt of the damage. Nearly 26% of the state's student enrolment (200,000) was displaced. Not only were children forced from their homes, but a number were separated from their families. In some cases it took half a year to reunite students with their families (Fagnoni, 2006: 4). In a 2009 Congressional Hearing, Louisiana's State Superintendent of Education, Paul Pastorek, reported that 'by September 2005, every state in the nation had received at least one hurricane-displaced student and 12 states had received more than 1,000' (Pastorek, 2009).

As a result of this movement, schools and education authorities across the country were impacted. The United States education structure is highly localized. Standardization is disparate, in everything from enrolment procedures to paperwork for students with Individual Education Plans (IEPs). Accordingly, schools had an incredibly difficult time absorbing students in large numbers. In some cases, information on grade level or IEPs was lost completely. Only limited information was housed at the state level and when a glut of requests for information came in, the Louisiana State Department of Education did not have the capacity process them. The type of documentation mentioned above is crucial for both assigning students in age-appropriate groups as well as administering, when necessary, a variety of support services. In addition, when federal funding was made available to schools to support displaced students, this paperwork was essential to secure the money. Even in the instances where paperwork was accessible, it did not exist in readily transferable formats and in one location (ibid.: 1–2). For students with special needs coming from New Orleans, IEPs were filed locally in hard copy and washed away in the floods.

While the impact on the education system of the city as the whole is compelling, the experience of individual schools, students and practitioners offers a further level of complexity and understanding. For instance, the educational responses of primary and secondary schools differed from those of institutions of higher education. By January 2006, the city's major universities reopened (Katz, 2006c: 1). With the city's primary and secondary schools, only 15% had resumed normal operating functions by February of the same year (Katz, 2006b: 1). At the one-year anniversary, less than a third of schools had been reopened (Liu et al., 2006: 6).

A Micro Perspective on the Educational Response

Hurricane Katrina was a devastating force for the city of New Orleans' public school system. In the wake of the flooding, 64,000 students were displaced and damage of approximately $800 million was incurred to school buildings and property (Steele et al., 2011: iii). Concerning the latter, 80% of 439 school buildings from 127 different schools suffered more than 25% damage (New Orleans Public Schools: Facilities Master Plan, 2010: 1). It is important to remember that even though water recedes, the damage done even by a few inches can bring an entire edifice to the ground. Some areas of New Orleans were flooded by as much as six metres of water. Important to note is that even these statistics were compiled solely from schools within the Orleans Parish School Board (OPSB). They exclude schools from the neighbouring parishes of St Bernard and Jefferson and ones that are privately funded. These school authorities also served students from the city.

Skipping forward to six years after the storm, New Orleans has become the epicentre of a national debate surrounding the leadership and structure of publicly funded schools. In the spring of 2010, 61% of the 38,000 public school students were enrolled in an independently administered and open enrolment school (ibid.: xiii), a major transformation, compared with the situation before Katrina. Indeed, as schools reopened after the Hurricane, more than half did so with a changed status, enabling them to be run independently (Carrns, 2006). Referred to more commonly as Charter Schools, the decentralization of hiring and revenue responsibilities grants school leaders more autonomy in the everyday running of the 'school house':

> Charter Schools are publicly funded elementary or secondary schools that have been freed from some of the rules, regulations and statutes that apply to other public schools, in exchange for some type of accountability for producing certain results, which are set forth in each Charter School's charter.
>
> (National Education Association, 2011)

For the champions of the school reform movement, this has been a tremendous victory in limiting the powers of what is viewed as a traditionally large and ineffective school bureaucracy. Today, New Orleans has the largest proportion of Charter Schools for a city in the country.

For others, changes to the system have been mired in controversy. The shroud of disapproval exists on two main issues. First, in the year prior to Katrina, the State of Louisiana underwent the process of taking over a majority of the schools from OPSB. Under conditions from the Federal Governments' 'No Child Left Behind Act' (NCLB), the state is meant to take control of schools that are deemed to be failing through repeated weak performance on state-designed standardized testing. The state entity in Louisiana is known as the Recovery School District (RSD), 'prophetically' named as such prior to 2005. Some disagree with the intervention of the state into local decision-making. The second and more hotly debated reason surrounds OPSB's treatment of its practitioners immediately following the storm. Prior to Hurricane Katrina, OPSB contracted an independent consulting firm, Alvarez and Marsal, to aid in the implementation of a number of school budget cuts. After Hurricane Katrina, Alvarez and Marsal recommended that OPSB terminate all teacher and principal contracts. In addition to disenfranchising a large group of people who could help with the rebuilding of the city, the decision left many displaced people without a steady source of income. As justification, this was seen as an opportunity to 'cleanse the system'.

In a Masters dissertation, *Educational Responses to Flooding in New Orleans and Hull*, Newton (2010) documents experiences of key practitioners in both the immediate aftermath and time since Hurricane Katrina. On one level, there is the perspective of the long-term New Orleans educator who was displaced by Hurricane Katrina and subsequently relieved of administrative responsibilities. On another, there is the documented effort of those who have worked to rebuild the system from the ground up. For the most part, all agree that one of the biggest failures of school administration was central communication and the unfair treatment of teachers. A former tenured principal interviewed explained in clear terms that the only communication of termination came through an announcement on CNN and a final wired cheque he received at the evacuated location. When expressing feelings on the question of his firing, the principal stated that:

> It was a news blast and the guy representing Alvarez and Marsal said you need to get a job … I think it was highway robbery. It was thievery at the highest level. You had 6,000 employees that when a natural disaster occurs you just fire them all with no consideration of their families and lives and you set up to severance packages or assistance programs to assist them in finding homes … you're talking about a city of people who lost their homes and lost their family members and

all you do is tell the people who have been one year to 30 years, 40 years that there is no money coming.

(Newton, 2010: 49)

An appropriate rhetorical question raised subsequently by the principal is: 'How can a school system rebuild without the help of individuals likes the teachers, administrators, bus drivers and janitors who previously worked at these schools?' The point is furthered by the sentiment of those in neighbouring school districts that were not terminated following the storm. In these cases, many educators fought to come back and help rebuild.

In neighbouring St Bernard's Parish (SBP), the impression left by educators is that even in the face of extreme devastation, people felt a responsibility to return and help in the rebuilding effort. SBP rests just east of New Orleans, but was equally devastated by the flooding. As many as 15,000 homes remained unoccupied in SBP three-and-a-half years after the storm (Liu and Plyer, 2009: 2). A smaller school district, SBP operated 14 schools that worked with 8,800 students (St Bernard Parish School Board, 2010). Newton's work reveals that the sentiment of those involved was more resilient as they felt connected to helping the rebuilding effort.

Following the storm, recession of floodwaters and assessment of damage, the RSD was charged with the primary task of rebuilding the school district after the OPSB ceded control. This reconstruction officially began in April 2007. The autumn of 2007 represented the first official reopening of the city's schools. In this effort, many obstacles were necessary to troubleshoot. For example, with the destruction of the majority of the system's infrastructure, the RSD needed to erect 7,000 modular classrooms. In buildings that were salvageable, school officials also had to renovate a number of spaces, including bathrooms and kitchens.

The district was also forced into the position of re-hiring approximately 600 teachers during the summer of 2007. Some former OPSB teachers refused to 'reapply' for previously tenured positions. It is in this vacuum that organizations such as 'Teach for America' (TFA) have been able to grow. TFA trains new teachers who consist primarily of recent college graduates and places them in some of the most high-risk schools nationwide. While only 15 TFA corps members taught in 2006 in Greater New Orleans, the number grew to about 100 in 2007, and 200 in 2008. Finally, with regard to funding provided for the rebirth of New Orleans schools, the school district received an approximately $80 million grant from the Federal Emergency Management Agency

(FEMA). Needless to say, this money evaporated quickly. The rebuilding of schools is a process that is projected to take well over a decade. An interesting point to note is that when Langston Hughes Academy opened in August 2009, it was a school that was the first publicly reconstructed building after Hurricane Katrina.

When debating the role of greater autonomy among New Orleans schools, there are both practical and pedagogical considerations to take into account. On a practical level, greater autonomy within the schoolhouse has allowed the school district to focus on larger issues of reconstruction. The city has now become open to new models of teaching and learning, such as the Knowledge is Power Program (KIPP) and the New Tech Network. Both of these Charter School systems have incorporated innovative practices in classroom management and the use of technology respectively. They have given options to parents who may want different learning environments for their children.

To provide a flavour of what all of the above has meant for individual schools: the Recovery School District demonstrated an intention to act quickly against schools deemed to be failing by repurposing leadership and curriculum. This includes some of the city's most historically recognized institutions. Built in 1958, George W. Carver High School's sixty-five acre campus, which included a feeder middle and elementary school, was submerged under ten feet of water following Hurricane Katrina (Pepper et al., 2010: 41). As one of the more storied schools in the city, Carver possesses an extremely strong alumni base. However, this support has been 'entangled in the struggles endemic to the New Orleans – and Louisiana's – public school system, including its chronic underperformance, racial achievement gaps and troubled governance' (ibid., 2010: 36). After Hurricane Katrina, Carver was included in the 107 of the 127 OPSB schools that were absorbed by RSD (ibid.: 38). While some of these schools, like John F. Kennedy High School, were closed due to low re-enrolment and severe facility damage, Carver was moved to modular classrooms on the fields behind the skeleton of the old structure and placed under new leadership. Carver High School first reopened after Hurricane Katrina in the fall of 2007. Initially not a designated Charter School, Carver operated under a number of district mandates including the implementation of scripted reading programs. Since 2007, Carver has failed to make significant gains with its student population. After the 2011 school year, the school's performance score of 44.8 out of 200 rested well below the District average of 69.2 (Recovery School District,

2011). Furthermore, with a graduation rate of only 55.7%, it was ranked the fourth lowest performing non-alternative high school in Louisiana. As a result, the RSD has deemed that Carver will either 'be transformed into a Charter School or phased out and replaced by a new Charter School' (ibid.). For many long-time supporters of Carver, the potential for an entirely new school located on the campus half a century after it first opened has left some alumni up in arms and extremely disappointed. Nevertheless, this 'transformation' reflects a clear effort by the RSD to act quickly against schools that are deemed academically unacceptable. It is a further endorsement of the district on behalf of Charter Schools.

Prior to Hurricane Katrina, it would have been considered glib to title an editorial on New Orleans education 'Lessons from New Orleans', a caption that was indeed used by the *New York Times* on 15 October 2011 (New York Times, 2011). Nevertheless, there are a number of reasons to acknowledge and embrace the changes that have occurred:

> In 2003, the majority of students attended schools that were academically unsatisfactory and only 28% of students attended schools that met state standards. Public schools in Orleans Parish have made significant progress, which has accelerated post-Katrina, and now 68% of students in Orleans attend schools that meet state standards.
>
> (Plyer and Oritz, 2011: 36)

Even though these statistics demonstrate dramatic improvements, there are still a number of areas for development that should be highlighted. The first is more anecdotal, in terms of the fact that more people need to 'buy' into the system. The existence of so many Charter Schools within the city remains a political hot topic. Some critics would go so far as to say that Charter Schools create a form of institutional segregation in New Orleans. While Charter Schools are open enrolment, the application process for each unit is by choice. For some, this means that non-Charter Schools become 'dumping grounds' for students who do not have proactive individuals acting on their behalf. That said, many of the Charter Schools within the city are active with marketing and recruitment.

Second, there needs to be more consistency in the quality of education across the city. Since the flooding was so devastating, many of the schools that were established after the storm were rushed into creation to meet the needs of all of the returning children. In addition, budget cuts have limited the number of social workers and counsellors to school sites. Greater consideration should be given to the psychological wellbeing of students returning from the storm. However, to succeed in this realm requires a tremendous amount of manpower and planning.

Finally, plans need to be put into place in the event of a future disaster. The primary educational response to Hurricane Katrina has been simply to rebuild the school system from scratch. There needs to be a strong plan in place to educate students and families, protect important paperwork and information on students, and build structures that are more resilient to enduring future events.

Conclusion

From an outside perspective, the change that the education system in New Orleans has undergone as a result of Hurricane Katrina and the flooding of the city has been nothing short of drastic. If the New Orleans Charter School experiment succeeds, a potential new model will be set for how to administer large urban public school districts. The case also demonstrates the significant disruption that can be caused by natural disasters. With a structure as highly decentralized as the United States education system, Hurricane Katrina highlighted the immobility of students and their records.

Through this chapter's discourse, an attempt has also been made to generate a further insight into a broader understanding of global flooding, the importance of education in disaster response, and some of the personal struggles it takes to rebuild and come back stronger than before. From this information, educational researchers should raise the question of what can be learned of value from studying cases such as the one surrounding Hurricane Katrina. First of all, it is clear that not all responses to natural disasters can be the same.

Serious attempts should be made by educational researchers and emergency planners to limit generalizations across cases of flooding. What has been discussed above concerning New Orleans may not apply, for instance, to the flooding scenarios in Hull and East Yorkshire from the summer of 2007 (discussed in Chapter 5) or the most recent Japanese tsunami (a focus of attention in Chapter 8). It is therefore important to search for areas of enduring and value and understanding.

In this respect, the first step is to 'identify the boundaries between a phenomenon and its context' (Yin, 2003, 13). Here is where the work of

Bereday (1964) offers important insight. Bereday believed in a total in-depth study of a case before evaluation and assessment can be made. Since qualitative research provokes interpretation, 'conclusions must be treated with considerable caution' (Phillips and Schweisfuth, 2006: 91). Bereday himself wrote that, when details are not prioritized, even the smartest individuals can make unreasonable generalizations. For instance, researchers who do not understand the cultural implications behind a foreign language can make such errors:

> Such mental blinkers, surprisingly worn sometimes even by the highly educated, are the greatest obstacles to true international understanding. In a large number of cases, wrong judgments are caused by an inadequate knowledge of the language of the country under analysis.
>
> (Bereday, 1964, 132)

When thinking about New Orleans, the growth of Charter Schools and the decentralization of local school authority should not be taken as a sign that this would be good practice everywhere. What made sense for the city in the wake of Hurricane Katrina was the need to delegate as many key decision-making responsibilities as possible, such as faculty hiring and curriculum design. In regions of the world with a dearth of qualified human capital, perhaps this path should not be recommended. The United States has, in significant part, been able to support rebuilding nationally through Federal and philanthropic sources. Such funds may not be available in other parts of the world.

Even though this chapter has been limited in the scope of its exploration, it sets a basis for future research. There will be enduring value and merit in continuing to question (as illustrated below under 'Questions for Further Consideration') the educational response to Hurricane Katrina. One important aspect that can be abstracted from the discussion above is that the presence of capable individuals matters. Whether in the design of schools or in the response to disaster, the presence of qualified practitioners can mitigate the potential for harm done to children. This is especially so when it is considered that, even five years after the storm, the battle to build back has still not been completed.

Acknowledgement

It is wished to acknowledge the feedback and support received from Dr Andrew Porwancher (University of Oklahoma) in the researching and writing of this chapter.

Questions for Further Consideration

1. How has increased educational attainment of students in New Orleans altered population demographics related to individual wealth?
2. What pedagogical reforms have lead to drastic improvements in student performance?
3. How did the firing and subsequent rehiring of teachers due to Hurricane Katrina impact teacher quality?
4. How have social and emotional needs of individual students been met or neglected by support services as they have returned to school?

Suggestions for Further Reading

1. For further general reading and lessons learned on the subject, the following is recommended: Fagnoni, C. M. (2006). *Lessons Learned for Protecting and Educating Children after the Gulf Coast Hurricanes*. Washington, DC: United States Government Accountability Office.
2. For anyone interested in learning more about Charter Schools, the influence they have had, and the role they have played in post-Katrina educational reconstruction, the following is recommended: Steele, J. L., Vernez, G., Gottfried, M. A. and Schwam-Baird, M. (2011). *The Transformation of a School System: Principal, Teacher, and Parent Perceptions of Charter and Traditional Schools in Post-Katrina New Orleans*. Santa Monica, CA: RAND Education.

References

Bereday, G. Z. F. (1964). *Comparative Method in Education*. First Edition. New York: Holt, Rinehart and Winston.

Brookings Institution (2005). *Hurricane Katrina Timeline*. Washington, DC: Brookings Institution.

Carrns, A. (2006). Charting a new course: after Katrina, New Orleans' troubled education system banks on charter schools. *Business*, 24 August. Online. Available at: online.wsj.com/public/article/SB115638176750244050-c9tcWeTmCrIAG10IXb5FZyikobw_20060922.html?mod=tff_main_tff_top [Accessed 2 December 2011].

Eggers, D. (2009). *Zeitoun*. San Francisco: McSweeney's Books.

Fagnoni, C. M. (2006). *Lessons Learned for Protecting and Educating Children after the Gulf Coast Hurricanes*. Washington, DC: United States Government Accountability Office.

Greater New Orleans (2010). *Teach for America*. Online. Available at: www.teachforamerica.org/corps/placement_regions/greater_new_orleans/greater_new_orleans.htm [Accessed 20 July 2010].

Heneveld, W. and Craig, H. (1996). *Schools Count: World Bank Project Designs and the Quality of Primary Education in Sub-Saharan Africa*. Washington, DC: The International Bank for Reconstruction and Development/The World Bank.

Jonkman, S. N., Maaskant, B., Boyd, E. and Levitan, M. L. (2009). Loss of life caused by the flooding of New Orleans after Hurricane Katrina: analysis of the relationship between flood characteristics and mortality. *Risk Analysis, 29*, 5, 676–98.

Katz, B., Fellowes, M. and Mabanta, M. (2006a). *Katrina Index Monthly Summary of Findings: January 4*. Washington, DC: Brookings Institution.

—(2006b). *Katrina Index Monthly Summary of Findings: February 1*. Washington, DC: Brookings Institution.

—(2006c). *Katrina Index Monthly Summary of Findings: March 2*. Washington, DC: Brookings Institution.

Kersting, N. F. (2010). *Changes in Flood Management Strategies Over Time*. Paris: UNESCO. Online. Available at: www.unesco-ihe.org/Flood-Management-Education-Platform/Flood-Modelling-for-Management2/Changes-in-Flood-Management-Strategies-over-Time [Accessed 20 July 2010].

Lawshe, C. (2010). *Global Climate Change: Evidence*. Washington, DC: National Aeronautics and Space Administration. Online. Available at: climate.nasa.gov/evidence/ [Accessed 24 July 2010].

Liu, A., Fellowes, M. and Mabanta, M. (2006). *Special Edition of the Katrina Index: A One-Year Review of Key Indicators of Recovery in Post-Storm New Orleans*. Washington, DC: Brookings Institution.

Liu, A. and Plyer, A. (2009). *The State of New Orleans Three and One Half Years after Hurricane Katrina: An Overview*. Washington, DC: Brookings Institution.

Louisiana Department of Education (2005). *Grade 8 Test Results*. Online. Available at: www.doe.state.la.us/lde/saa/2166.asp [Accessed 20 July 2010].

National Education Association (2011). *Charter Schools*. Online. Available at: www.nea.org/home/16332.htm [Accessed 24 November 2011].

National Geographic Society (2010). *New Orleans: A Man Made Disaster*. Video. Washington, DC: National Geographic Society.

New York Times (2011). Lessons from New Orleans. *New York Times*, 15 October. Available at: www.nytimes.com/2011/10/16/opinion/sunday/lessons-from-new-orleans.html?_r=3 [Accessed 28 November 2011].

Newton, B. (2010). *Educational Responses to Flooding in New Orleans and Hull*. Masters Dissertation. Oxford: Oxford University.

Organization for Economic Cooperation and Development (OECD) (2006a). *France: Policies for Preventing and Compensating Flood-Related Damage*. (2006) Paris: OECD.

—(2006b). *Italy: Industrial Hazards Triggered by Floods*. Paris: OECD.

—(2006c). *Japan: Floods*. Paris: OECD.

Pastorek, P. (2009). *Hearing Testimony of Louisiana State Superintendent of Education Paul G. Pastorek: US Senate Ad Hoc Subcommittee on Disaster Recovery*. First Edition. Washington, DC: United States Senate.

Pepper, M. J., London, T. D. and Dishman, M. L. (2010). *Leading Schools During Crisis: What School Administrators Must Know*. Lanham: Rowman & Littlefield Education.

Phillips, D. and Schweisfuth, M. (2006). *Comparative and International Education: An Introduction to Theory, Method, and Practice*. First Edition. London: Continuum.

Plyer, A. and Ortiz, E. (2011). *The New Orleans Index at Six: Measuring Greater New Orleans' Progress Toward Prosperity*. New Orleans: The Greater New Orleans Community Data Center.

Recovery School District (2010). *New Orleans Public Schools: Facilities Master Plan*. New Orleans: Recovery School District.

—(2011). *Transformation Fact Sheet*. New Orleans: Recovery School District. Available at: rsdla.net/Libraries/Documents_and_Reports/Transformation_Fact_Sheet_-_Carver.sflb.ashx [Accessed 28 November 2011].

Rivers, D. (2010). *Bangladeshis Rely on Floating Schools Amid Flooding*. CNN. [Online]. Available at: edition.cnn.com/2010/WORLD/asiapcf/07/19/bangladesh.floating.schools/index.html?fbid=z13x NWE5V0p#fbid=RWI7oyBQlwA [Accessed 20 July 2010].

Sadler, M. (1900). How far can we learn anything of practical value from the study of foreign systems of education? In J. H. Higginson (ed.) (1979). *Selections from Michael Sadler*. Liverpool: Dejall and Meyorre.

Saint Bernard Parish School Board (2010). *Our Story*. Video. Chalmette: Saint Bernard Parish School Board.

Schleifstein, M. (2009). Study of Hurricane Katrina's dead show most were old, lived near levee breaches. *The Times-Picayune*. [Online]. Available at: www.nola.com/hurricane/index.ssf/2009/08/answers_are_scarce_in_study_of.html [Accessed July 20, 2010].

Sherman, S. and Shapiro, I. (2005). *Essential Facts About the Victims of Hurricane Katrina*. Washington, D.C.: Center on Budget and Policy Priorities.

Shriver, M. K. (2009). *Interim Report*. Washington, DC: National Commission on Children and Disasters.

Sommers, M. (1999). *Emergency Education for Children*. Boston: Mellon-M.I.T. University Program on Non-governmental Organizations and Forced Migration.

—(2003). *The Education Imperative: Supporting Education in Emergencies*. Washington, DC and New York: Academy for Educational Development and Women's Commission for Refugee Women and Children.

Steele, J. L., Vernez, G., Gottfried, M. A. and Schwam-Baird, M. (2011). *The Transformation of a School System: Principal, Teacher, and Parent Perceptions of Charter and Traditional Schools in Post-Katrina New Orleans*. Santa Monica: RAND Education.

Stockholm International Peace Research Institute (SIPRI) (2011). *SIPRI Military Expenditure Database*. Online. Available at: milexdata.sipri.org [Accessed 24 November 2011].

Time (2010). A calamity waiting to happen. *Time*. Online. Available at: www.time.com/time/covers/20050912/gulf_coast_map/ [Accessed 20 July 2010].

United Nations Educational, Scientific and Cultural Organization (UNESCO) (2010). *EFA Global Monitoring Report 2010, Reaching the Marginalized*, Table 11: Commitment to education: public spending. (Paris, UNESCO). Available as an online database at: gmr.uis.unesco.org/ [Accessed 24 November 2011].

Winthrop, R., Ndaruitse, S., Dolan, J. and Adam, A. (2010) *Education's Hardest Test: Scaling up Aid in Fragile and Conflict-Affected States*. Washington, DC: Brookings Institution.

Yin, R. K. (2003). *Case Study Research: Design and Methods*. Third Edition. London: Sage Publications.

5 Floods in the United Kingdom: School Perspectives

Kevin Beaton and David Ledgard

Chapter Outline

Introduction

This chapter describes the impact upon, and experiences of, two Hull and East Riding of Yorkshire schools flooded in 2007. Hull is a major port. The city of approximately 260,000 people is located and has developed over time on the confluence of the narrow River Hull and the major estuarine River Humber. The fact that Hull is so located, and a maritime city, would perhaps lead the reader to surmise that threat from flooding was foreseeable. This is only partially correct. The 2007 floods were not caused by tidal pressure from estuarine rivers. They were the consequence of an unprecedented (and therefore completely unanticipated) deluge of incessant rainfall over a short time period. Therefore the story that will be told here is of the kind of emergency for which, perhaps not unreasonably, there were no significant, directly relevant, contingency plans, from the perspective of schools affected.

The narrative comprises first-hand descriptions of the experiences of two schools: Croxby Primary School and Sidney Smith (Secondary) School. It will provide insights into what they encountered, and how they responded – for the most part having to make things up as they went along. It will show how they were supported, but also where they were left to struggle on their own. It will shed light on the both the immediate, but also the longer-term, impact of the floods, not only on the schools as institutions, but on pupils, teachers and communities. The opportunity will also be taken to look for lessons: what could have been done differently with the benefit of hindsight, and what was done correctly. Also described will be some of the systems and procedures that have now been put in place to prevent or reduce the consequences of a similar event, were it to be repeated in Hull and the East Riding of Yorkshire. These actions may also have relevance for other contexts. To add directness and to try to convey a sense of what it must have been like 'at the chalk face', the two case studies are presented in the first person singular: through the voices of the two school headteachers: David Ledgard and Kevin Beaton.

Case Study 1: Cottingham Croxby Primary School – David Ledgard

'Day One': Monday 25 June

Cottingham Croxby Primary is a school for children aged 4 to 11 years situated almost on the boundary between the city of Hull and the adjacent village of Cottingham. With thirty-five years of experience in senior management, twenty-three as a headteacher, I thought I had encountered just about every sort of problem or challenge that can arise when running a large primary school. However, on the morning of 25 June 2007, I discovered how ill-prepared I was for the sudden and far-reaching, devastating effects of a major flood. The area in and around Cottingham is flat and, as a native of the area, I had clear knowledge of there being no similar occurrence within the previous fifty years in the Hull area. The rainfall on the day of the flood was heavy and continuous and followed on from an above average amount of rainfall on the previous weekend that had resulted in a back-up of one set of toilet drains, quickly sorted by the school caretaker.

However, on the day of the flood, it very soon became apparent that the water was building up at an alarming rate and creeping towards the main entrance of the school building and very soon we were experiencing water slowly seeping in through the main entrance and also through the doorway of Classroom 6. As the caretaker and the deputy headteacher began to sweep and vacuum the water up, I rang a parent who had a large on-board water pump in his van, which he used to clean carpets. I hoped he could assist us with the removal of water from the building. However, within a very short time, it was obvious that we were fighting a losing battle, and being mindful of the safety of all those in school I decided at 9.25 a.m. to evacuate the building.

Using the school phones and a number of staff mobile phones, we began contacting parents, many of whom then offered to contact other parents, neighbours, workmates and relatives. Within a remarkably short period of time we were able to reach all but a handful of parents. Through 'the grapevine', parents began to arrive at school to collect their children, and although it was contrary to normal protocols, following kind offers from parents to take children other than their own, I made the exceptional decision to allow children to leave the premises for their own safety. The parents volunteering to take children were relatives, friends, neighbours or workmates and had contact numbers for the children's parents. The fact that Croxby Primary School functions as a close-knit community was crucial in this regard.

At this stage I also sent home members of staff who were in the greatest danger of being marooned, as we were receiving reports of other areas around the city being cut off. The remaining staff were then employed in the task of saving as much equipment as possible including: lifting the very valuable school piano onto blocks; gathering up electrical items, ensuring that the main school server was raised above the water level; and stacking books, papers and other important materials on table tops to keep them dry. Within a short time the staff who had already left were telephoning back, giving us more detailed first-hand information of the extent of the flooding both in and around Hull and warning us to make for home as soon as possible because many roads were closed or inaccessible due to flooding.

As the water levels continued to rise, the whole school became flooded and we gathered the remaining few children into the school hall to sit above the water line on the stage, supervised by staff until such time as they were collected by parents. Incredibly, the word of our plight had spread so quickly and effectively, the last remaining child was picked up and left the building at

10.30 a.m. The remaining staff except myself, the caretaker, the chairman of governors and his wife were sent home at 10. 45 a.m.

As the caretaker began to secure the building I sat in my office, sitting shin-deep in water, telephoning the Local Authority (LA) – the East Riding of Yorkshire Education Authority – to get help and advice, while wondering whether or not I would get an electric shock from either the telephone or the water, as all the power sockets were under water. To this day, no one has ever explained to me why that does not happen. My contact with the LA proved frustrating and unhelpful, as they were totally unprepared for the scale of the disaster and overwhelmed by the demands for help across the county. I left the building mid-afternoon, along with the caretaker, chairman of governors and his wife. I then turned my attention to rescuing my own family who were spread around three different parts of the county. I only grasped the enormity of the situation when I saw the extent of the flooding on the television.

'Day Two': Tuesday 26 June

The rain had stopped, but the whole site remained under water. There was still no contact or support from the Local Education Authority. However, in what proved to be an important development, on this second morning, I was invited to participate in a live local radio show 'talk-in'. The presenter enquired how I was coping with the devastation of the school. I explained the extent of the damage, described the difficulties being experienced by children, staff and families and touched upon my frustrations with the Authority and their lack of understanding and support. Within twenty minutes of the broadcast, a council lorry arrived with two workmen carrying a very small ornamental pond electric pump capable of pumping about 25 gallons per hour! It was only when they asked where they could plug it in that the futility of their request and the enormity of the situation became apparent. This incident served to speed things up, and later that afternoon a very large diesel pump was delivered to the site. Within twenty-four hours, 12,000 gallons of water had been pumped off the site. However, this had virtually no effect upon the level of the water. It took several days of pumping throughout the day and night to clear the surface water completely.

Throughout this time, the chairman of governors, school business manager (SBM), caretaker and a handful of staff were on site to identify ways of communicating with children and parents to update them of the situation. Without telephones, computers, printers, materials and a base, we were extremely limited and hampered in our attempts to keep people appraised of the situation and – more importantly – the future of the school. We were kept fed and watered by a group of parents and staff who plied us with food and hot drinks. Although staff were keen to come into school and help clear up, we were unable to let them on site until all the water had been pumped away and the building had been made safe and secure. At this stage, staff imagined that the damage was confined to a small ingress of water. It was to be some time before they witnessed the extent of the devastation.

'Day Three': Wednesday 27 June

Following an emotional visit to the site by a local headteacher, such was his concern for our plight that he made the supreme gesture of offering us a base at his school. He returned to his school and immediately cleared his own office, prepared a meeting room for our daily use, and organised an additional phone line for us to use, for as long as needed. This was our first major offer of support, three days into the crisis. With help from one of our governors in the LA procurement department, we also acquired four mobile telephones, increasing our ability to contact our audience more quickly and effectively.

The First Few Weeks

It took several days of pumping before we eventually reached the stage where we could enter the building, and it was the first opportunity for us all to meet as a staff since the day of the flood. Being mindful of the extent of the devastation, I warned the staff to be prepared to shed tears as they toured the school seeing the fruits of their labour ruined. I suggested that they walk around the school individually to absorb the horror of the situation and then meet together near the staffroom in half an hour. Many tears were shed during that time and when they eventually made their way back to the staffroom, where I appraised them of the seriousness and hopelessness of our situation. I still remember the massive awakening and enormous sense of responsibility that I faced when a member of staff responded loudly and spontaneously with the definitive statement: 'We will get through it because you will lead us through it together'. That responsibility served as an immense impetus to carry me through the many dark and frustrating days ahead. We were, of course, not the only members of our school community suffering. Many families were also experiencing serious and unexpected financial hardship, having to find money for additional childminding due to the school being closed and, even worse, not having the money to pay for the additional supervision because they were not able to work, as their place of employment was out of action due to flood damage. Many of the families are still repaying the large debts that were accrued during the flood recovery period.

The day after the offer from our neighbouring headteacher, we moved into Bacon Garth School (2.6 kilometres away from our own campus) and thus began the first major part of our revival. This incredible act of kindness and understanding was without doubt the single most important factor in giving us the strength and the belief to work towards a positive outcome, regardless of the problems that we might encounter. It served to give us the determination needed to find a venue to house the children temporarily until the end of term, while investigating the feasibility of rebuilding the school. We felt that, in spite of the difficulties and inappropriateness of the venue, it was essential to remain as one in order to keep the spirit of the school together.

We were not only rebuilding the school but also rebuilding lives and trying to keep the spirit and ethos of the school alive and together. After intense pressure from myself and the chairman of governors, the head of a nearby high school offered to house our Year 6 children. We accepted, but after two weeks I withdrew the children as they were suffering from their separation from the rest of the children and asked to be removed, preferring to wait for a solution where the whole school population could be accommodated. It thus became apparent in the earliest stages that the need to keep the whole school population together was essential and that, as children and parents alike stated, 'we could achieve anything as long as we stayed together'.

In the absence of any further solutions suggested by the LA, the SBM and I set about exploring every large venue in Cottingham and the surrounding areas. After having investigated several possibilities, we realised the enormity of our task. However, through a contact of one of our governors, we were invited to explain our needs to the site manager at the University of Hull, 2.1 kilometres away. This resulted in our second major offer of support. In an act of great kindness, we were invited to occupy the whole of the ground floor of a Faculty. The SBM and I then had to assess the feasibility of all aspects of getting the children to and from the site and the practicalities and dangers of working, not only in an adult-designed building, but also cohabiting an adult site and environment. Health and safety and wellbeing issues needed to be thoroughly examined, thought through, and risk assessments needed to be drawn up.

The University staff were extremely helpful and supportive and made numerous amendments to their normal working policies in order to facilitate our needs. We contacted all local transport companies, but as they were already committed to school runs, we were only able to secure their services from 9.15 a.m. onwards when they had finished their contracted duties. Equally, they needed to collect our children earlier in the afternoon in order to ensure that they were back in time to do their normal afternoon runs. Although this meant a shortening of the school day for us, it was infinitely better than no schooling, and more importantly it gave us the first opportunity to reunite the whole school population, which I felt was a pivotal step on our road to recovery.

Having acquired a base and transport we then approached the landlord of the public house situated across the road from the Croxby School campus, to ask for assistance with our transport plans. He was eager to assist and offered us full use of the car park as a safe and convenient picking up and dropping off point for all the buses. We informed the local police and traffic wardens of our plans and the possible disruptions to traffic, and they also responded in a very positive and supportive way by assuring us that they would be on hand at the crucial times to cone off and control the traffic flow. Having until now, received very little help and encouragement from the LA, the positivity, no matter how small, from the University, the public house landlord and the police was a massive boost to our confidence and served to increase our determination to get the school back together again as soon as possible.

Our school population is made up of approximately 60% of children who live outside the immediate vicinity of the school and most of those pupils arrive by car. Moreover, in view of the fact that a large number of our local families had been displaced as a result of the flooding, this added to the volume of traffic around the site, raising the levels of risk to the children.

Moving the school population of 320 pupils and forty teachers and teaching assistants needed a constant shuttle of double-decker buses. The organisation of children, parents, buses and traffic was a major challenge that needed military-type precision to ensure the safety of all parties. Once we had drawn up and approved the plans we then needed to share them with parents and children.

Yet again, communications were the key to success. The combination of an army of leaflet-delivering parents, the use of the school website and terrific support and publicity from all the local media sources enabled us to reach all families to appraise them of developments. Having completed risk assessments for the journeys and the accommodation, taking account of the inappropriateness of the building for children, we then started our occupation of the University.

The first morning was a very emotional but happy event, as parents, children and staff reacquainted themselves and regaled each other with their own particular experiences and hardships. However, the overriding feeling of warmth and pleasure at being back together raised everyone's spirits and provided a boost for the next phase of our revival. Due to the regular warm and friendly responses from everybody at the University, we very quickly settled in and began to enjoy our time there. To the children it represented warmth, security and routine, particularly for those who were displaced from home or experiencing change and great hardship within the home due to flood damage. In addition to the school bond, we felt part of the family within the University boundaries. The whole experience was positive and represented a great adventure to many of the children, giving them a rare glimpse and understanding of University, which hopefully may spur them on to return at some time in the future as part of their life-long learning. It also gave them a routine that was stable, welcoming and familiar, which in turn promoted a strong sense of togetherness and wellbeing. We finished our stay at the end of the Summer Term with a mock degree ceremony where I presented every child and adult with a 'Croxby' Honorary Degree. This effectively completed a most memorable chapter in the history of the school.

In parallel to all of the above, and not forgetting our flooded campus, the need to rebuild the school became a strong common focus for everyone, as many staff and families were also experiencing hardships and displacement as a result of the flooding of their homes. Some were struggling within their own homes in damp, damaged and restricted conditions, while many others were displaced, existing in a variety of temporary placements including caravans; rented houses and flats; friends' and relatives' homes; hotels – even sheds and garages. This fragmented and disrupted existence further served to unite the whole school community and created a determination to stay together whatever might happen. The school community represented hope and comfort for these people and a building would enable families to begin to experience some aspects of normality and security. Children and parents said that they were happy as long as we were together and that they had every faith in our ability to arrive at a successful conclusion.

Immediately following the clean-up there was a very frustrating period of inactivity when the Local Authority halted progress while they investigated the feasibility of re-building the school. In fact their initial plans were to demolish the school building and disperse our pupils to other local schools. I then found my time taken in co-ordinating a strong lobby against these proposals and I am still very proud of the campaign that we launched to save the school and will be forever thankful to the many parents, friends and politicians who helped us in our endeavours. The local media also played a massive role in promoting our case into a much wider public domain. After a very harrowing time where the future of the school hung in the balance, the LA relented and contractors were engaged to re-house the school population on the school field while simultaneously rebuilding the original school building. I emphasised to the LA that our wish was to stay together and be on our own school site and a plan was drawn up to accommodate our request.

Several weeks after the flood event, following a comprehensive appraisal of the flood damage, insurers gave the go-ahead to gut the building and plans were drawn up to rebuild completely the inside of the school. Contractors then began the enormous task of clearing up and disposing of the mass of materials and equipment. After years of being thrifty and instinctively salvaging almost every kind of materials, it was very hard to agree to the wholesale disposal of most of the equipment. It was also very emotional seeing so much equipment being thrown away that was either very personal or had taken years to acquire. Seven large containers were placed on the playground and any books, stationery and general school equipment that had not actually been in the water was stored away in the containers. I needed to be at my most acquisitive in securing a knock-down deal for 1000 large plastic storage containers from a local manufacturer to be used to store all the small loose materials.

The Next Few Months

During the summer break the rebuild commenced. The school field was dug up and then tarmacked and eight Portakabin classrooms, two blocks of outside toilets and a large administration unit were erected. The SBM, the administration team and I put in many hours of time sourcing and acquiring all the necessary equipment needed for the temporary classrooms in time for the new term – by no means an easy feat.

Contractors occupied the school building except for three classrooms and a corridor that, because of a different floor construction, were ready for use. A large metal fence was erected to ensure the safety of the children and staff, and to demarcate the building work from the temporary school buildings. Fortunately we have two entrances to the school and were therefore able to redirect the parents to the new operating entrance while the contractors used the entrance on the other side of the campus.

Within the temporary accommodation arrangements I had a very small office made at the end of the corridor, originally created for my use to conduct confidential discussions. However, with the high levels of stress and strain upon all individuals within the school, it very quickly became used for people who were feeling the strain and needed somewhere private to share their worries and concerns and weep. It became known as the 'Crying Room' and throughout the nine months of our enforced exile was used by many, many people. During the rebuilding period, I myself spent most of my time based in a corridor alongside two other administrative colleagues. Although this put us all in the open and available to any and all visitors, it proved to be massively effective in not only supporting and helping me, but also in cementing the three of us as a very strong and unified team, which still exists to the present time. The combination of trying to run the school while also negotiating with builders, the LA and trying to equip a large school from scratch was the most challenging and stressful time of all.

As I had worked in an architect's office prior to coming into teaching I understood the rebuilding needs and processes which were not always appreciated by the LA who sometimes could not, or would not, want to find alternative solutions. However, the learned skills came in very useful, helping me to understand and visualise the myriad of issues, developments, possibilities and problems associated with such a massive project. I was being severely challenged on a daily basis, having to make decisions for and about the school, the building, the staff, children, parents, the media and the local community. I had to operate at a level above and beyond the expectancy and remit of a headteacher.

The task of restoring the school to its former glory while also taking every opportunity to improve and develop the building, coupled with the complex job of equipping the school with all the necessary books, furniture, materials and vital equipment needed, was proving very challenging for myself and the SBM. For instance, the paperwork and invoices for the insurance claim ran into hundreds of items, amassing a bill in excess of £350,000. The final reconciliation took many months to finalise and was a gargantuan task for the SBM, without whose dedication, resilience and skills we could not have come through so successfully.

After nine months of intense building activity, noise and constant challenges to the contractors and us, refurbishment began to draw towards completion.

As soon as the classrooms were ready, the builders invited us to bring in the stock and equipment that had been stored away since the flood. To our horror, the containers were not fully waterproof or airtight and all the papers, books, clothing kits and perishable items had rotted away and were of no use. Insurance assessors condemned everything and we had to start from scratch, yet again, at very short notice in order to be ready for our official reopening ceremony: Easter of 2008.

On taking over the building again, the interior had been transformed and brought us right back up-to-date with the types of equipment and resources needed for the twenty-first century. It was in effect a 'new' school placed within our old building. The only things that remained the same were the roof and the exterior walls. The effect on the staff and children was tremendous. They walked around admiring every aspect of the school and immediately felt back at home, happy, proud and contented once again.

The experience showed the pride and resilience of our whole community and left us with incredible memories but created a bond that will last forever. We did it by doing things together and each helping the other when the going got tough. As I reflect upon the success of the whole episode I realise that the dedication, loyalty and support given to me so willingly by so many people, in particular the SBM and the chairman of governors, was without doubt the single most important factor in us achieving our goal. Without their help, I could not have achieved what we have today. We each have unique and treasured memories of the experience and all feel immensely proud to be connected with Croxby School.

Case Study 2: Sydney Smith School – Kevin Beaton

The Flood and Immediate Aftermath

Sydney Smith School is an 11 to 16 age-group mixed comprehensive school. Its 2007 population comprised 1,515 students and 177 staff. The school site is situated in and owned by the East Riding of Yorkshire Council despite the fact that it is a Hull School. The weather events described above for Croxby School also had a devastating effect at Sydney Smith School: 104 ground floor rooms in the school flooded to a depth of around four feet. The final cost of repairs totalled around £5.8 million.

There had been a considerable amount of rain in the week preceding the flood and the morning of Monday 25 June 2007 was marked by continued heavy rain. On arrival at school, I was informed by the site staff that they had deployed some sandbags at the rear of the site as there was some water starting to drain from the farmer's fields at the back of the school and onto our site. The vast majority of the students travelled to school on 16 school buses. Despite moving the students as quickly as possible into the school, they were all drenched and soaked through to the skin. The bus drivers also reported that the roads leading into the school were starting to become impassable as they began to flood. At the same time, the school started to receive telephone calls from parents who were bringing their children to school by car who reported that they would not be continuing the journey as the roads were starting to flood.

Although it was only 9.00 a.m., and the school had only been open for around 45 minutes, it was very clear that the situation was deteriorating to such an extent that all the staff and students would have to be evacuated from the school site. All schools have plans to deal with emergencies such as fire or bomb threats that would require evacuation from the school buildings and assembly at some mustering point within the school grounds. These procedures are well known and rehearsed at least once a term. The situation we were confronted with on the day of the flood was different in that it required the evacuation from the school site. In addition, the vast majority of the students were not within easy walking distance of their home. The first problem was ensuring that the parents were aware of our decision and that the students could get back safely either to their own home or another one of a relative or a friend. Most of the students had mobile phones. This expedited the process, and very quickly the vast majority of parents or relatives were contacted and gave permission for their child or children to make their own way home. The staff at the school ensured that all the students were in groups as they left on their respective journeys. There were a few students whose parents asked us to keep them at school until they could be collected from there. It proved fortunate that the decision to close Sydney Smith School was made so early as, later in the morning, the number of people accessing the mobile phone networks caused the systems to temporarily stop working.

The Year 11 students were that morning taking their final GCSE Science examination and they were in the main hall and the two gymnasiums during the evacuation of the school. This would have been a disturbing time for them. They could obviously hear the noise as the rest of the school was being evacuated and they could also see that water was starting to seep in under the doors of the examination halls. I arranged that myself and the two deputy headteachers would each go to an examination hall in order to explain to the staff and students the arrangements for the end of the examination. I went over to one of the gymnasiums at around 9.30 a.m. At this time the water in the school grounds was about ankle deep. The GCSE Science examination finished at 10.30 a.m. The students had made contact with home, and the vast majority were able to leave the school site by 11.00 a.m. At this time, when I returned to the main block in the school, the water level in the school grounds had risen to mid-calf height. This was an indication of just how fast the water level was rising.

A number of school staff had received telephone calls from schools that their own children were attending as these schools were also making arrangements to close. Therefore as soon as the students had all left the school site I made the decision that all the school staff could make their way home. My last message to them was that they should monitor their email accounts for further instructions. The site staff continued to work incredibly hard to try to stop the floodwater entering the ground-floor rooms but by the afternoon they were forced to abandon their efforts as it was clear that the task was futile.

On the following day, Tuesday 26 June, it was not possible to gain access to the school site as it was still flooded to a depth of two to three feet. However, the finance and buildings manager at the school, with remarkable foresight, went to a local supplies store and purchased an array of protective clothing in sufficient quantities for staff to wear during the subsequent clear-up operation. On Wednesday 27 June, school staff were able to gain access to the school by wading in through a foot of water. I made contact with the Local Authority and they made arrangements for the Fire Brigade to attend the school and pump out the still flooded areas. On this day, working with the finance and buildings manager and the deputy headteacher, plans were made for the partial reopening of the site, despite the flood damage to all ground-floor rooms.

By Monday 2 July, all staff were back on site as the ground floor of Unit 6, a four-storey building, had been cleared and cleaned by school staff which allowed staff, to enter the block and make use of the upper floors and rooms in the block. The following day, Tuesday 3 July, saw the return of the then Year 10 students who followed temporary timetables while based in the upper floors of Unit 6. By Thursday 5 July, the ground floors of Unit 3 and Unit 4 had also been cleared and cleaned so that the upper floor and rooms in the blocks could be used by Year 8 students who followed temporary timetables while based in the rooms. In both year groups the timetables had no practical-based subjects such as design and technology, art, or physical education.

By Monday 9 July, arrangements had been finalised for the Year 7 students and the Year 9 students to cover their last two weeks of the summer term up to Friday 20 July 2007. All the Year 7 students were to be taught at The University of Hull, nearly 10 kilometres away, in the Wilberforce Building. The University of Hull had been very supportive in this matter as they had also suffered some flooding in June 2007. Discussions with the University's director of facilities produced a licence that detailed the numbers of students and staff to be based at the University and the different responsibilities of both the University of Hull and Sydney Smith School. This licence was signed by both parties. The Year 9 students were based at another location in the city – the Gemtec Arena (a sports complex) – on alternate days to take part in different activities, but with the major focus on physical activities.

On Wednesday 11 July 2007, the school finally received confirmation from the Local Authority that they would support the full repair and reinstatement of Sydney Smith School on the current site. Five days later, project directors and contractors were appointed in respect of the civil works to be undertaken. The next day a meeting was held with these parties. Decisions were made about the priorities for the reinstatement and return of the different buildings and rooms. The day after the school closed for the end of the summer term, on Saturday 21 July, the school site was designated as a building site and it moved under the control of the contractors. It remained under their control until they had completed working on particular building units, at which point each unit would come back under control of the school. During the summer break, over 400 men worked on the site around the clock, for seven days a week. Six weeks later, by the start of September 2007, the work that had already been completed would otherwise have taken 6 months, following normal working routines.

During the summer break, the school administrative staff undertook the enormous task of replacing all the damaged books, furniture and equipment so that school could open again in September. At the start of the new term in September, Sydney Smith School had 19 temporary classrooms, a temporary hall and four sets of temporary toilets erected, plumbed in and connected to the electrical system. There were also ICT facilities accessible in all the temporary classrooms. The school had weekly 'Contract Progress Meetings' with the project director and contract manager right up until the work was completed. These meetings would sometimes be attended by Local Authority staff who always received copies of the minutes. The final handover to the school took place in May 2008, around 11 months after the flood occurred.

Impact on Students

At the start of October 2007, the school conducted a survey of all the families then in the school to try to measure the impact of the floods in the community. Table 5.1 shows the responses received from 1365 families.

The survey revealed that around 20% of all the students then at the school had been displaced in some way from their normal living arrangements. For these students they had the double pressure of having disruption at school and at home as well for most of the academic year 2007–8. The attendance at the school showed a slight dip before resuming its previous upward trend. The number of students classified as 'Persistent Absentees' (PAs) also rose in 2007–8 before resuming a downward trend, as Table 5.2 shows.

There was no clear evidence that behaviour was any different from previous years but for most of the academic year 2007–8 Sydney Smith School was designated a building site or partial building site that required much greater supervision from staff than would be usual. There were three particularly striking issues that I personally noted about how the floods affected the

Impact	Year 7	Year 8	Year 9	Year 10	Year 11	Overall School
Living upstairs	7%	4%	5%	5%	7%	6%
In Caravan	8%	5%	7%	4%	7%	6%
With Grandparents	1%	1.5%	1.5%	0.5%	1%	1%
With other family	1%	1%	1%	2%	1%	1%
Hotel	0.5%	0.5%	0.5%	0%	0%	0.2%
Temporary renting	3%	1%	3%	4%	2%	4%
No Impact	68%	36%	38%	48%	42%	46%
No response	11.5%	51%	44%	36.5%	40%	35.8%

Table 5.1 Impact on Students

Year	2006–7	2007–8	2008–9	2009–10	2010–11
Attendance as percentage of total enrolment	88.76%	**88.2%**	90.06%	89.6%	91.3%
Percentage of students classified as 'Persistent Absentees'	12.01%	**13.3%**	10.3%	8.3%	6.6%

Table 5.2 Impact on Attendance

students at the school. First, there were a number of students, particularly those in Year 7 and Year 8, who became upset and nervous when there were further occurrences of heavy rain. Secondly, there was the impact on their circle of friends outside of school, as many were dispersed from their usual homes into temporary accommodation. This often broke long-standing friendships on a temporary basis. The final point related to how many students did not want to share their home experiences with the school. This is also reflected in the number of families who chose not to respond to the school survey even though the school was aware that in some cases they had been affected by the floods.

There would have been some impact on the educational attainment of the students who were taking their GCSE Science examination at the time the flood was occurring, but it would most likely only have been marginal, as the students were taking the final module in a series of examinations and no student was noted to have achieved significantly less than expected. The real academic impact occurred with the students who were in Year 10 at the time of the floods in 2007 and who subsequently sat their examinations at the end of the academic year 2007–8. I had been warning that this would be the case from immediately after the floods in June 2007. These students had a disrupted summer term at the end of their Year 10 and had restrictions placed on them throughout virtually the whole of their time in Year 11. Additionally, during the floods, they lost coursework in a range of different subjects that they had completed in Year 10. They were told by the examination boards that they had to repeat this work during their Year 11. This student cohort was also denied access to full facilities in a number of subjects. By way of examples: in ICT, the facilities were badly disrupted and the reinstatement was not complete until May 2008; dance students had no access to any specialist facilities and were based in a classroom until May 2008; all Year 10 Design and Technology work was lost in the floods and students were not able to start any practical work until December 2008. The only special consideration given by the examination board was a short extension to the deadline for completing coursework. The examination results for the students at Key Stage 4) in 2007–8 were a great disappointment and significantly below what students would have been expected to have achieved. The examination boards are allowed to make up to 5% improvement in results for when and where special circumstances arise. In the case of Sydney Smith School, apart from in Art, they chose to make no allowance for the Year 11 students generally in the school.

Impact on Staff

When the floods had subsided there was a real determination from the staff to get the school back open for business again, and they willingly took on tasks that would not usually have been within their remit. Coincidentally, just before the floods, Sydney Smith School had been selected to close in August 2015, under the Hull 'Building Schools for the Future' programme. Everyone understood the importance of getting the school to admit students again.

Once the new school year started in September 2008, all staff faced disruption to their normal working environment, with the amount of temporary accommodation and the school being a partial building site. As different parts of the campus were handed back to the school there were complex logistical arrangements to be made to achieve the move back into the permanent facilities.

There was undoubtedly an increase in workload for staff as many resources developed over the years had been lost in the floods and not all lost resources were replaceable for the start of the new term in September. The uncertainty over the timing of any moves from the temporary accommodation also complicated the planning of lessons, as it was more of a challenge to plan practical lessons in temporary classrooms. There were also a number of staff who, as well as dealing with the additional workload and stress at the school, were also facing difficulties caused by flooding in their own homes. In many cases, these were problems that would take much longer to resolve than the repair work at school. In such circumstances it was an amazing show of resilience and resolve by many of the staff who were determined to make the school a place of stability for the students.

Conclusions and Lessons

What comes across especially powerfully from all of the above is that a 'strong' school is more than a building and the people who occupy it. A strong school is a 'community': something rather more intangible, but nevertheless fundamentally important. It is this vital community element that is in danger of being shattered irrevocably by disaster, but it is also the same element that can be the critical factor in helping schools to pull through.

To emerge successfully from a disaster ordeal takes strong, resolute leadership and teamwork, with considerable resourcefulness to look for creative solutions. Good organisational, interpersonal communication skills are essential and the ability to nurture, support and inspire people is constantly needed. Good publicity can have a massive impact on the nature of outcomes. Success in handling and engaging the media requires good contacts and an ability to put the school forward and to articulate the issues.

With regard to specific lessons learned and changed practices, Sydney Smith School now has agreement from every family on how their child should get home in the event of the school ever having to be evacuated. This information is logged on the student school file and means that the school can now be evacuated without having to make individual contact with each family. The school had intended to make contact with staff through email but the school computer systems had been disabled when the computer server room flooded. The school has now developed a disaster management plan that will allow a similar situation to be managed and allow communication with all staff. The school computer servers are now at a height that should avoid them flooding. The back-up security tapes were damaged when the safe that was fireproof but not waterproof was flooded, so the safe is now where it will not be affected by a future flood. There has been a flood prevention plan developed. This has resulted in a large trench dug at the back of the school to ensure any water that runs off the field is taken away from the school into an appropriate soak-away.

The Local Authority ensured that all the drains on the school site were cleared and the school now has a regular programme to ensure they are clear at all times. Sydney Smith School had many difficult and unproductive discussions concerning special consideration for the Year 11 students in the 2008 GCSE. As the examination boards do not seem to have any flexibility in their systems, a lesson appears to be that any appeal should deal only with individual students.

A significant number of Sydney Smith students benefited from counselling work carried out as part of a University of Cumbria research project in 2007 (see 'Suggestions for Further Reading' below). As a consequence, the school has established a Parent Services Team. This provides a more focused family support that includes, among other things, work on emotional wellbeing. Working with other professionals to manage all the aspects of the reinstatement and refurbishments made the school review its planning processes. These have consequently become much more systems based and more solutions focused.

Croxy Primary School now has flood gates stored on site to protect each door opening. A depth sensor, which is linked to the main school alarm system, has been fitted in the main sewer to warn of any dangerously high level of water building up in the sewer. The school now has a school emergency evacuation and contact plan.

> ## Questions for Further Consideration
>
> 1. What emerges from these case studies that is more generalizable and what remains context specific?
> 2. Would 'School Clustering' arrangements, posited in chapter 1 as a strategy worth considering, have had any relevance or practicality for the stories told here?

Suggestions for Further Reading

Two qualitative research projects emanating from the Universities of Lancaster and Cumbria looked at the recovery response of adults and children to the Hull 2007 floods. Several interesting publications have emerged directly including:

1. Whittle, R., Walker, M., Medd, W. and Mort, M. (2011). *Flood of Emotions : Emotional Work and Long-Term Disaster Recovery. Emotion, Space and Society.* (In Press).
2. Walker, M., Whittle R., Medd, W., Burningham, K., Moran, Ellis, J. and Tapsell, S. (2010). *Children and Young People 'After the Rain has Gone': Learning Lessons for Flood Recovery and Resilience: Final Project Report for 'Children, Flood and Urban Resilience: Understanding Children and Young People's Experience and Agency in the Flood Recovery Process'.* Lancaster: Lancaster University. Available at: eprints. lancs.ac.uk/49462/1/FINAL_REPORT.pdf [Accessed 5 December 2011].

References

Coulthard, T. J., Frostick, L., Hardcastle, H., Jones, K., Rogers, D., Scott, M. and Bankoff, G. (2007). *The 2007 Floods in Hull. Final Report by the Independent Review Body, 21st November 2007.* Hull: Hull City Council.

Lancaster University (2011). *Hull Floods Project.* Website. Available at: www.lec.lancs.ac.uk/cswm/ Hull%20Floods%20Project/HFP_home.php [Accessed 5 December 2011].

Earthquake in China: A Sichuan Case Study

Zhou Zhong

6

Chapter Outline

Introduction

On 12 May 2008, a devastating earthquake of Magnitude 8 struck the regions of Sichuan, Gansu and Shaanxi Provinces in south-western China. The earthquake killed 88,000 people, injured 400,000, left five million homeless, and affected the lives of 45.6 million across an area of 500,000 square kilometres. This chapter will examine how the education sector responded, both during and after the earthquake, at national to regional levels, and with special reference to three themes – school safety; psychological healing; and cross-regional support. The chapter will conclude with a summary of key lessons and ongoing challenges.

Background to the 2008 Great Sichuan Earthquake

China is one of the most natural disaster-prone countries in the world. Due to its climatic and geological locations, China has to face each year almost all types of natural disaster, with the significant exception of modern volcanoes. Among them, the most frequent and widely distributed in China are meteorological disasters such as flood and drought, and geological disasters such as earthquakes and mudslides. Today, 70% of cities and 50% of the population of China are located in areas prone to natural disasters. Each year, according to data for the period 1990 to 2008, natural disasters affect an average of 300 million of China's population, leave nine million homeless, and cost over 200 billion Yuan (US$30 billion in 2011) (State Council, 2009). In recent years, in the context of global climate change and rapid economic development and urbanisation, pressure on the ecological environment is increasing, with consequently greater risks from natural hazards.

On 12 May 2008, during an early Monday afternoon, when almost all children were at school and adults were at work, an earthquake with a Magnitude of 8 on the Richter scale struck in the densely populated mountainous Wenchuan County in Sichuan Province in China. What then followed was further battering from a series of frequent aftershocks, storms, floods, landslides and mudslides. By 25 August 2008, figures had emerged to indicate that the earthquake had killed 88,000 people, injured 400,000, left five million homeless, and affected the lives of 45.6 million across an area of 500,000 square kilometres comprising 417 counties in ten provinces. Fifty-one counties in three provinces of Sichuan, Gansu and Shaanxi were designated as the most severely affected areas, covering an area of territory of 132,596 square kilometres and a population of 20 million (State Council, 2008a). The earthquake also caused extensive damage to basic social infrastructure, including damaging 12,000 school buildings in Sichuan Province and 6,500 school buildings in Gansu Province, disrupting schooling of 2.5 million children (UNICEF, 2009a). On 30 August 2008, two days before the start of the school year, a second earthquake measuring 6.1 on the Richter scale struck Sichuan and Yunnan Provinces along the same fault line as the Sichuan-Wenchuan earthquake, resulting in dozens of people perishing and hundreds more injured.

The Chinese government, civil society and international organisations responded with rapidity and strength. Hours after the first strike, the Chinese

Premier Wen Jiabao arrived at Dujiangyan, a city less than 100 kilometres from the quake's epicentre at Wenchuan County, to oversee massive disaster rescue and relief, operated around the clock. During the same evening, the Government of China commenced a top-grade national emergency response, the first of its kind since 1949 (Gov.cn, 2008a). Thousands of volunteers, many of whom were young people taking leave from their study or work, arrived on the same day of the earthquake or soon afterwards. Among those volunteers were also groups of experts consisting of the best researchers and planners in China. Rescue teams from Japan, Russia, the Republic of Korea and Singapore also began operations on 16 May. This was the first time foreign rescue teams had taken part in disaster relief in China since 1949 (ibid.).

Ten days after the earthquake, 21 provinces and municipalities across China were mobilised by the central government to form 'one-to-one' twinning arrangements with severely damaged counties to support comprehensive relief and reconstruction (MCA, 2008). A month after the earthquake, the State Council of China issued a circular to confirm and expand the one-to-one cross-regional twinning. The twinning would last for three years and involved comprehensive assistance in terms of resources and services for emergency relief and reconstruction (State Council, 2008a).

On 19 September 2008, four months after the main earthquake, the State Council issued a master plan: 'State Overall Plan for Post-Wenchuan Earthquake Restoration and Reconstruction' (State Council, 2008b). This set the goal of completing, in three years, the recovery of basic livelihood and socio-economic development, either to the same levels or above those that existed before the earthquake. The main reconstruction targets involved: safe accommodation; stable employment; basic public service, such as compulsory education and medical care; improved infrastructure and eco-environment; and strengthening capacity in disaster prevention, risk reduction and environmental protection. At the time of writing (December 2011), the master plan has been translated into massive recovery and reconstruction actions, notable for their remarkable speed, scope of mobilisation and resource inputs. All of this can be seen as a reflection of the strength and determination of the Chinese government and society to achieve a powerful, effective and efficient recovery from such a great catastrophe.

Emergency Response in Education

The term 'emergency response' is used here to refer to the first three months of emergency rescue and relief after the main earthquake, and while frequent aftershocks still took place.

Restoring Access

The earthquake damaged one out of every seven schools in Sichuan Province, making the restoration of access to education an urgent priority under the slogan of 'no child left behind by the earthquake' (Sichuan News Agency, 2008). The education sector's immediate emergency response in the first week was to rescue people, collect information for needs assessment, and make plans to restore schooling. At the same, time, government and communities from local to national level began to mobilise resources for relief and rehabilitation. Two days after the earthquake, the Ministries of Finance and Education of China provided an emergency fund of 50 million Yuan (US$ 7.8 million) to support educational recue, rebuild schools and restore teaching and learning (Xinhua, 2008a). In addition to government funding, local and regional governments in quake-affected areas and social organisations across China also conducted a wave of media campaigns to raise funds for educational and socio-economic relief and reconstruction. Additionally, the Chinese government, social organisations and international organisations all contributed trained personnel for educational services, and facilities and materials for teaching and learning to quake-affected regions.

Within the first two weeks after the earthquake, different types of temporary schools were reopened gradually for those in most need. Priority was given to students in their final year of primary or secondary schools, because national college entrance examination and graduation and progression examinations are all held in June and July. Many severely damaged areas sent all or at least part of their final-year upper-secondary school students to restart classes in neighbouring towns and cities and where there was a degree of increased relative safety (Zhang, 2008). Meanwhile, many severely affected areas also reopened classes for final-year students in primary and lower secondary schools in temporary local schools.

By 1 September 2008, a total of 3.4 million students in all earthquake-affected areas in Sichuan, including 650,000 newly enrolled, were able to access an educational setting in time for the new school year (Xinhua, 2008e).

For those who returned to schools in their own locality, 33% of them returned to their undamaged original school buildings, 38% to repaired school buildings, and 28% to prefabricated classrooms or tents. Less than 1% moved to schools away from their own locality. The county-level governments in earthquake-affected areas also provided subsidies for living expenses to all students. For 51 severely and most-severely affected areas, 20,000 students left their home towns to restart schooling, 11,000 of them went to schools in 16 counties within Sichuan, supported by subsidies for living expenses from Sichuan provincial government, while over 8,000 students went to schools in 25 other provinces across China and received subsidies from their new schools.

Temporary schools in quake-affected regions took several forms. For example, some primary and secondary schools moved into an open space to make a large educational compound with prefabricated classrooms or tents at the edge of their town or city. Some schools moved into safe buildings in other towns in the same province or in neighbouring provinces, in newly built but unopened schools, prefabricated classrooms on a temporary campus space adjacent to local schools, or in buildings on college campuses. Some transitional schools operated for one month, while some others lasted two or three years. All these temporary schools occupied a relatively tight physical space, well-fenced, and with security arrangements in place. Within them were formed closely-knit teacher-student relationships (Zhang, 2009).

Special attention was given to ensure fair access to school for the most vulnerable groups. For example, the Ministry of Civil Affairs of China worked with UNICEF to establish a tracking system to identify orphans and monitor their ongoing situation. Targeted capacity-building programmes were also provided to safeguard these children's social welfare (UNICEF, 2009b). Six hundred-and-fifty children were soon confirmed to be orphaned by the earthquake and were provided with public subsidies and various social endowments to support their living and education. In addition, China Life Insurance set up a foundation to provide monthly support for all orphans until they reach the age of 18 (FT China, 2010). As of August 2011, the China Children and Teenagers' Fund has worked with UNICEF to raise 53 million Yuan (US $8.3 million) for children orphaned or disabled by the Sichuan earthquake, and has opened ten rehabilitation centres for those children in the ten most severely affected areas to provide at least ten years of education and care services (Sichuan Daily, 2011a). Many emergency measures for inclusive education such as these have now been incorporated into national planning for future emergency responses in education.

In the higher education sector, the Ministry of Education (MOE) adopted a series of emergency measures to ensure fair access and to increase opportunities for disadvantaged groups. One week after the earthquake, the MOE announced the one-month postponement of college entrance examinations for 120,000 students in severely quake-affected areas in Sichuan and Gansu provinces (Xinhua, 2008b). The MOE also provided learning and living subsidies to students preparing for those examinations in severely affected areas, college scholarships for students orphaned and disabled by the earthquake, and free and open access to secondary vocational schools. Moreover, over 1,400 higher education institutions outside Sichuan added a 2% recruitment quota for Sichuan students. Institutions in Sichuan also allocated 20% of their total recruitment quota for students from quake-affected areas. Universities and colleges also provided national and institutional subsidies to support about 35,000 students whose families were affected by the earthquake (Xinhua, 2008d).

Healing and Child Protection

Another major challenge to emergency relief was to provide prompt and appropriate healing measures to help the quake-affected children and their parents and caretakers to cope with trauma, especially in the worst-affected areas where children and adults alike were displaced to live in temporary shelters and thereby exposed to increased risk of abuse, neglect and danger. It was thus a vital undertaking to help children to build up long-term capacity to revive hopes and dreams.

Psycho-social support was provided with the arrival of the first groups of rescue and relief workers, days after the Sichuan earthquake. However, many healing services were at first provided in a sporadic and uncoordinated manner, often by unqualified volunteers or professionals with little field experience in emergencies. Many qualified education and medical professional groups and organisations did provide leadership to set up systematic registration and reporting measures for psychological interventions, but it took time for them to set up and operate (Xiang et al., 2008).

Child Friendly Spaces, an initiative that was set up in July 2008, was among the first-implemented and most effective and sustainable models to provide integrated psycho-social support and protection services in and after the earthquake (Sichuan Online, 2011). Co-developed by UNICEF and China's National Working Committee on Children and Women, the Spaces were set up in camps and temporary shelters to provide a package of community-based services concerning child protection and psychological support in the most severely affected communities. Equipped with toys, library books, sports equipment, furniture and prefabricated structures, the Spaces delivered a diverse range of activities: daycare for pre-school-aged children; non-formal education for school-aged children; life-skills training for adolescents; and support for parents, caretakers and communities in general on core issues such as health, immunisation, injury prevention and child protection (UNICEF, 2009b).

Moreover, the Spaces also functioned as a network of knowledge centres for local expertise building. They operated with a uniform set of guidelines and service manuals and provided extensive training to teachers, social workers and volunteers, as well as community leaders working in the Spaces. Based in the Spaces, UNICEF and its Chinese counterpart also reached out to the wider communities through public campaigns to raise awareness of and improve measures on child rights and child protection issues (NWCCW, 2009).

In the first year after the earthquake, 40 Spaces had been opened in 21 counties in severely affected areas. In the three-year period to May 2011, 330,000 children benefited from them. The Spaces have become extremely well known places in quake-affected areas, and since 2010 they have been transformed from emergency initiatives to permanent institutions to serve their communities under the support and supervision of village or township governments (Sichuan Daily, 2011b).

Another successful model of psychological counselling services was provided by the School of Psychology of Beijing Normal University (BNU). Since the second day after the earthquake, BNU has provided over three years of psycho-social services to those severely affected. One week after the earthquake, BNU had already put forward a package of coordinated strategies to address the challenge of psycho-social healing for quake-affected areas. As a leading national centre in psychological education research and education, BNU worked with the Office of the National Disaster Reduction Commission to set up a specialist committee for Sichuan earthquake response. The Committee conducted needs assessment in the earthquake zone, to inform both the provision of psycho-social support and policy making. Meanwhile, it also set up a national hotline to provide psychological support and information services to those who needed them (People's Daily, 2008).

Moreover, on 20 May 2008, BNU also published an urgently needed self-help guidebook (BNU, 2008c) and group counselling guidebooks for primary and secondary schools respectively (BNU, 2008a, 2008b). These books formed a solid foundation of healing and capacity-building resources for countless professionals, volunteers, teachers and students to address disaster trauma across China. No less importantly, teachers and students form BNU also provided over three years of direct counselling services through building a network of 14 fully-equipped counselling centres. These benefited 700 local teachers and a large number of students in severely affected Deyang prefecture.

In psychological support and in other aspects of emergency response in education, the China National Institute of Education Sciences (NIES) also played an important role. The NIES dispatched several groups of experts to conduct field research and provide services in teacher training, psycho-socio support and planning for school rebuilding (NIES, 2009). The NIES also coordinated with educational authorities and academic communities, from the national to local level, to develop and implement state planning for post-earthquake reconstruction in the education sector.

Education Reconstruction and School Safety

The promulgation of the State Overall Plan for Post-Wenchuan Earthquake Restoration and Reconstruction, on 19 September 2008, four months after the main earthquake, marked the transition from emergency rescue and relief to systematic post-earthquake reconstruction. In effect, responses during and after emergencies thus operated on a continuum.

National Planning in Education Reconstruction

The State Overall Plan put forward five main strategies for education restoration and reconstruction (State Council, 2008b):

1) An education revitalising project in quake-affected regions: to restore and reconstruct infrastructure for educational institutions at all levels and all types, with a special emphasis on nine-year compulsory education; and to coordinate enterprise-run institutions and non-government institutions in education.
2) The restoration and reconstruction of high-quality buildings for primary and secondary schools; the expansion of enrolment in boarding schools and the proportion of boarding students; and the mobilisation of teachers from other regions to teach in quake-affected primary and secondary schools.

3) For rural areas: a decision to locate general upper secondary schools and secondary vocational (technical) schools in county centres; lower secondary schools in villages and towns; and to make a relatively concentrated distribution of primary schools.
4) Rationalisation, through reconstruction, of the location of kindergartens and schools for special needs.
5) Recovery and restoration of damaged higher education institutions and research institutions.

Public infrastructure such as schools and hospitals became the first priority in post-earthquake restoration and reconstruction. In particular, China determined to make schools the safest of all public buildings (China, 2008).

Three-and-a-half years after the earthquake, the MOE reported that education in all the quake-affected areas had been restored to conditions that were at least the same, and in many areas better than, the pre-earthquake level (Guangming Daily, 2011). According to data available in October 2011, 99.5% of 8,323 planned schools in 142 quake-affected counties have been completed. Among them, 99% of 3,001 planned schools in 39 nationally designated most severely and severely affected counties have been completed (Xinhua, 2011).

National Initiatives on Building Safer Schools

There is no doubt that shortcomings in school safety severely exacerbated loss of life in the Sichuan earthquake. Many shoddily built school buildings were severely damaged in the earthquake. Some collapsed instantly. Large numbers of students and teachers were buried. According to a 21 May 2008 assessment of the Sichuan government (Bjnews, 2008), 13,768 schools in Sichuan were damaged by the earthquake, accounting for over 46% of all schools in Sichuan. Furthermore, 11,687 (85%) of damaged schools required reconstruction; 6,851 students and teachers were confirmed perished, accounting for 12% of the total death toll of 55,239; 1,274 teachers and students were missing and 8,810 were injured. The final death toll of students was reported as 5,335 but that of teachers has never been confirmed (Xinhua, 2009b). The earthquake devastation to schools incited a wave of national uproar over school building quality (CE Weekly, 2008; Finance & Economy, 2008). After much reluctance, the Government of China admitted 'possible quality problems' of school buildings damaged in the Sichuan earthquake of September 2009 (Gov.cn, 2009).

As physical infrastructure restoration and reconstruction proceeded with speed and at scale in quake-affected areas, one year after the earthquake, in

May 2009, the Government of China launched a three-year 'Safer School Project' chaired by the Chinese premier (MOE, 2009a). The overall goal was to make every single school building in China – over two million buildings in 400,000 primary and secondary schools that hosted 200 million students and 13 million teachers – 'the safest public place in China'. In fact, since as far back as 2001 and until the time of the Sichuan earthquake, the Government of China had implemented, in turn, three major projects to refit and rebuild school buildings in rural areas across China. However, despite these initiatives, buildings considered at risk still existed in many areas, especially in underdeveloped rural areas.

The Safer School Project proceeded in three steps: thorough assessment and planning; raising standards and planning; and refitting and rebuilding. In the first stage, in June 2008, less than a month after the earthquake, China launched a national survey to build a detailed monitoring database on safety conditions of every school building in China, with especial attention given to pre-2001 facilities. With regard to raising standards, in early October 2008, the MOE worked with UNICEF to dispatch on a study tour to Japan a delegation of policymakers and technical experts to learn about best practices in emergency preparedness and risk reduction (UNICEF, 2009b). Then, on 24 October 2008, the MOE, the Ministry of Housing and Urban-Rural Development (MHURD), and the National Development and Reform Commission jointly issued the 'State Guidelines on School Planning and Construction for Post-earthquake Reconstruction' (MOE, 2008c). These new guidelines gave detailed guidance on how to: choose school location; design, construct and assess the earthquake resistance of school buildings; retrofit vulnerable buildings; and develop safety standards for construction projects. In particular, the new guidelines substantially raised school building standards for rural areas, with special attention to schools in high-density rural areas where the earthquake risk was of Magnitude 7 or above. The scale of the task was estimated to involve the refitting and rebuilding of 400 million square metres of school buildings (27% of the total number).

On 24 June 2009, the MOE and ten other ministries jointly issued plans for action and supervision, supported by a technical guidebook for the Safer School Project (MOE, 2009b). According to June 2011 figures, the central government has provided 18 billion Yuan (US\$ 2.8 billion) for this project and another 20 billion Yuan (US\$ 3.1 billion) to construct new boarding schools across China. Regional governments have also provided matching funding to a power of ten, for two projects (MOE, 2011). As an overall result, the Safer

School Project has raised direct investment in school buildings, from national to local levels, to unprecedented levels.

Capacity Building on School Safety in Schools

In order to guide systematic emergency response for schools and educational authorities at all levels, in September 2009 the MOE put forward a revised version of the Education Sector's *State Plan for Rapid Response to Public Emergencies Resulting from Natural Disasters*, based on lessons and experiences from the Sichuan earthquake (MOE, 2009c). The Plan adopted a new classification of public emergencies; specified responsibilities and actions in risk prevention and emergency response, to be taken accordingly at national to school levels; and set up new systems to report information and mobilise emergency response materials.

In terms of curriculum development, China launched extensive national training programmes to build up institutional and individual capacities in school safety. On 1 September 2008, the first day of the new school year, the MOE worked with China Central Television (CCTV) to air a TV programme on natural disaster prevention, preparedness and response. Over 200 million school students in China were required to view the programme and all parents were also recommended to watch it. Since then, the programme has been developed into an annual 'first class in school' series on disaster prevention and reduction.

School safety education has also now been incorporated into the mainstream school curriculum and the professional development of teachers, in connection with psychological wellbeing and life-skills education. However, several challenges have persisted, which can also be traced back to the pre-earthquake period. The greatest challenge is that China still lacks a holistic and systematic approach to disaster education within the school curriculum. Disaster education covers a wide range of knowledge, skills and competences beyond the reach of a single subject-based course in China's national curriculum. At present, elements of disaster education exist in practice, such as: the optional module on natural disasters and their prevention in geography; safety education and mental health in moral education; and life-skills in sport and health (Zhang and Wang, 2010).

Another major challenge is a lack of stimulating methods in the teaching and learning of disaster prevention and reduction. This is mainly because the current curriculum provides too much emphasis on knowledge, and neglects skills development. The curriculum is also mainly transacted through lecture, book and paper-based examination. The lack of multimedia learning resources and pedagogical diversity leaves little space to motivate students and to take practical initiatives that actually impact upon daily life and emergency response behaviour (Ma and Feng, 2008). A third challenge concerns the lack of disaster education offered outside classrooms and schools, resulting in no reinforcement of what is taught in the classroom.

Consequently researchers have recommended that China should adopt an inter-disciplinary, multimedia and learning-by-doing approach to integrate disaster education with education on sustainable development and to permeate it into the teaching and learning of all compulsory courses (Zhang et al., 2011). In research literature on disaster education, Japan has frequently been cited as an excellent example, and other effective international practices have also been studied (Xue, 2008; Tan et al., 2010; Quan and Li, 2011). However, to effect changes of this kind will require time and political commitment to upgrade the national curriculum and create a national culture of disaster prevention and reduction.

Education Reconstruction and Cross-regional Support

Cross-regional Twinning Scheme

Within the first month after the earthquake, and following two mobilisation initiatives by the central government, 20 regions formed one-to-one cross-regional twinning arrangements with 18 severely affected regions in Sichuan, one in Gansu and one in Shaanxi. Within this overall scheme, nearly all sectors in the supporting regions twinned with their counterparts in quake-affected areas. By following state guidelines for cross-regional twinning (State Council, 2008a), the supporting regions shouldered the responsibility to provide comprehensive support of personnel, materials, funding, knowledge and technology to assist their respective recipient counties to restore basic living conditions and recover socio-economic development, while also receiving survivors from the quake-affected areas to their own regions and providing them with adequate education and training, medical treatment or employment.

Reconstruction priorities were given to residences and basic social services such as schools and hospitals. Other assistance tasks involved making direct investment, setting up entrepreneurship programmes and operating basic infrastructure. The supporting regions were partly supported by the emergency relief and reconstruction funding provided by the central government, and partly supported by their own funding. The direct materials support was required to be no less than 1% of the regional revenue in the previous year.

Improving Education Quality through Twinning

Within the general framework of region-county twinning, every school in severely affected counties was required to form one-to-one twinning with large and strong schools in their supporting regions. The twinning was especially important to provide rapid and increased access to vocational education. This sector not only faced the immediate challenge of restoring access, but also suffered from long-term capacity and quality of education challenges. The earthquake affected the education of 260,000 students in 209 vocational secondary schools in 51 severely quake-affected counties. At the beginning of the new school year in September 2008, cross-regional twinning helped to transfer over 77,000 of students to enrol in large and strong vocational schools in supporting regions and helped graduates from those schools to find employment in local enterprises (Xinhua, 2008e).

In the three years of post-earthquake education reconstruction, the twinning process has continued to make concerted efforts to increase access and improve quality of education, mainly through focusing on school planning and construction, teacher training, school twinning, internet-based educational resources sharing and joint research. The supporting regions in the twinning arrangements provided the major part of reconstruction funding.

To provide further insights to quite what was involved and achieved, the twinning arrangements between Jiangsu Province and Mianzhu County in Sichuan will be examined in greater detail by way of notional example. However, two other very successful twinning arrangements that should at least be acknowleged (and about which more information can be found, through the references at the end of this chapter), include: the twinning arrangements between Shanghai and Dujiangyan County in Sichuan; and twinning arrangements between Beijing and Shifang County in Sichuan.

The total funding for Mianzhu's 83 school and kindergarten reconstruction programmes was 1.8 billion Yuan (US$ 281 million). Jiangsu Province alone provided 1.4 billion Yuan (US$ 219 million), or 78% of total funding, to undertake 64 programmes, while the central government provided 1.5% of total funding. Other major funding resources were 12% from Chinese and international social organisations and individuals and 7% from the Chinese Communist Party (Mianzhu Online, 2011). In addition to the provision of direct funding, Jiangsu also helped Mianzhu to raise over 20 million Yuan for student scholarships from various philanthropic organisations in Jiangsu and other parts of China.

By the start of the spring term in February 2010, over 50,000 Mianzhu students had been able to move from temporary prefabricated classrooms to permanent new schools. All new schools in urban and rural areas were constructed in accordance with a uniform set of high standards in design, construction and equipment. They were all also fully equipped with science laboratories, computer classrooms, music classrooms, and other facilities that had never been seen before by people in rural areas in Mianzhu. This meant that, for the first time, Mianzhu removed urban-rural disparities in school facilities. Moreover, 74 high-standard schools from 13 municipalities and seven most-developed county-level cities in Jiangsu twinned with all schools in Mianzhu. The twinning provided comprehensive support centred on teacher development, including, among others, over 100 professional development initiatives that benefited all 3,231 teachers in Mianzhu. Furthermore, 119 Jiangsu teachers took short-term posts in teaching, administration and psycho-social counselling in Mianzhu (Deyang Daily, 2011).

Thus through twinning assistance of this kind, severely quake-affected areas have not only been fully restored but have made impressive leaps forward, in quality of education, in terms of both infrastructure and teaching and learning. Even though the officially designated region-county twinning initiative officially came to a close three years after the earthquake, a huge ongoing legacy remains. Twinning heritages such as trained teachers, school twinning relationships that continue under their own initiative, jointly-run educational institutions, shared e-learning resources and newly built schools all continue to contribute to the sustainable development of quake-affected areas.

Key Lessons and Ongoing Challenges

Key Lessons

There are a number of important experiences and lessons worth learning and sharing with the rest of world. First of all is the way in which the Government of China provided strong leadership at the national level to coordinate international, regional and local support in emergency recovery and reconstruction. The state guidelines on post-earthquake reconstruction issued by the State Council in September 2008 provided a strategic plan that involved all relevant government departments and which was supported by comprehensive scientific and technical expertise. The plan was rigorously translated into action, achieving a balance of both quality and efficiency. During the implementation process, the government also put forward a wide variety of complementary and reinforcing policies to help direct investments and support recovery efforts. With support from the academic community, social agencies and international organisations, the Government of China was able to align effectively many of the emergency-response programmes with upstream policy initiatives, and develop them into national policies, guidelines and standards that can benefit the whole country. This was especially true of disadvantaged groups and areas of China and those more vulnerable to future emergencies.

Secondly, regional government across China played a crucial role in the concerted efforts of emergency relief and reconstruction. As a long-held tradition in China, to address regional development disparities, developed provinces and municipalities in eastern China were mobilised to set up one-to-one twinning arrangements with severely damaged areas to provide emergency resources and services, including the design, construction and operation of many basic social services. This arrangement bypassed the intermediary bureaucracy, and created a healthy competition that promoted effectiveness and efficiency-based on measures well-adjusted to local conditions.

Thirdly, international organisations played an important role in emergency relief and reconstruction. The Sichuan earthquake triggered, for the first time in recent history, a request by the Government of China for international assistance. Within the first month after the earthquake, over 150 countries, regions and international organisations provided funding, experts and other emergency resources to the quake-affected regions. During the three-year reconstruction period, international organisations such as, UNICEF, UNEP, the World Bank, the Red Cross and Red Crescent, to name but a few, have worked continuously with their counterparts in China to provide relief and reconstruction resources and services. Among other things, this has contributed to the knowledge base and evidence-based policy development from the national to the local level. In particular, international organisations have helped to ensure that children and other 'most vulnerable' groups in the remote and isolated communities in the earthquake zone received equal if not even better benefit from rebuilt public services.

Lastly but no less importantly, the dedication of civil society has enabled a multi-stakeholder response to emergency relief and reconstruction, in every aspect and at every stage of recovery and reconstruction. This has helped to raise wider and longer public awareness of disaster-risk reduction. According to official registration figures, more than a million volunteers have contributed to the earthquake relief and reconstruction. There were also countless self-organised volunteers who worked on site and across China to raise aid, donate blood or provide other services needed for the quake-affected areas. The spirit of volunteering has become a national 'morality' in the context of building a harmonious society. Moreover, the expert community, many of whom also worked as volunteers, not only provided massive practical design, implementation, recovery and reconstruction efforts, but they also promoted public advocacy in China and globally to strengthen the capacity, as well as the culture, of disaster resilience.

Ongoing Challenges

Despite all of the above, challenges remain. Although the three-year national reconstruction plan was declared completed in September 2011, it remains imperative to maintain the reconstruction momentum, to strengthen education and development in general in a sustainable way, especially in quake-affected areas. A major challenge is for China to make disaster risk-reduction a national priority, and address it together with socio-economic development with political commitment and financial resources at many levels. The 2010–20 National Guidelines for Educational Reform and Development, put forward in 2010, included 'safe education and life-skills education' among strategic themes. More-focused policies, financial resources and trained personnel are needed to design and implement disaster risk-reduction in the education sector, in addition to continuing to construct safe school buildings. With regards to curriculum development and disaster risk-reduction, it is important to address integration and diversity in terms of both the content and methods of teaching and learning, in formal, informal and non-formal education. Moreover, it is imperative to engage and influence a broader range of decision-makers in government, the expert community and civil society on education for disaster risk-reduction.

Promoting fairness and equity is a challenge exacerbated by disasters. The severely damaged areas in the Sichuan earthquake had long been the least-developed areas in China. Their educational levels and all other aspects of socio-economic welfare lagged behind the rest of China. Children, women, the disabled and the elderly were the hardest-hit groups by the Sichuan earthquake. It is both important and necessary to use reconstruction processes as an opportunity to counteract pre-existing patterns of poverty, vulnerability and disadvantage on both in quake-affected areas and across China. However, there are often quality differences between pre-existing basic infrastructure and those newly refitted and reconstructed ones, such as the schools donated by supporting regions in most severely affected areas. Special attention is now needed to address access to the latter to ensure equity. In recent years, China has made ongoing reforms in education, health and other social welfare services. However, to create further momentum, it is worth exploring whether the resources and measures – such as emergency institutional and financial support to access to education and basic health care – that can be mobilised for emergencies can somehow also more routinely be accessed to promote long-term and consistent social welfare policies and initiatives. There is also an opportunity for the government to try to achieve even better coordination with a multitude of actors for more routinely provided social services. In other words, good practices that apply in emergencies can also be good practices in a non-emergency context and there is much to learn from, adopt and adapt.

Another major challenge is further to empower the local government and agencies in quake-affected areas through continued support from provincial and national governments. The goal here has to be to ensure that reconstruction efforts can endure, and newly built and better-quality infrastructure can be properly operated and maintained in order to serve the people for years to come. A further challenge to education and the public sector as a whole is information management. Public emergency management depends on timely and accurate information. For post-earthquake reconstruction in China, it is important to use information systems to monitor and evaluate the quality of ongoing efforts and evaluate their impact on the wellbeing of the affected populations. Moreover, China is a disaster-prone country with a rapidly emerging economy and changing society. As an act both to reduce disaster risk and to promote socio-economic development, it is imperative to develop comprehensive and transparent information management infrastructure and fully integrate it into policy-making and resource allocation.

Lastly, but no less importantly, there is another long-term challenge in respect of all-round teacher development. Teachers themselves were among the hardest hit groups in the Sichuan earthquake, although this has not received sufficient attention. During and after the earthquake, the teachers shouldered the role of protectors to their students and schools, but the teachers themselves were also victims who suffered from all kinds of losses: losses from which it takes a long time to recover. Essential to improving the quality of education, more psychological understanding and support is needed. Also required are more evidence-based policies and additional financial resources to ensure continuing professional development and socio-economic welfare improvement for teachers.

Questions for Further Consideration

1. What might be the potential, but also the limitations, of introducing one-to-one twinning initiatives as part of emergency recovery and reconstruction in education, in contexts other than China?
2. Which effective practices and challenges for teacher development described in this chapter do you consider to be context-specific to China and what insights might be more generalizable?

Suggestions for Further Reading

Most of the resource material accessed in researching this chapter takes the form of policy documents and media coverage. Unfortunately, much of this is only available in Chinese, despite where it is available online. Regrettably, some of the referenced reports which have played an important consultation role in government policy-making also have only restricted access status. To learn more about education and the Sichuan earthquake in China in the English language, readers are recommended to consult the English version of the following websites: the Chinese government (www.gov.cn); the Xinhua News Agency (www.xinhuanet.com); UNICEF China (www.unicef.org/china/); and the UN China (www.un.org.cn).

References

Beijing Municipal Commission of Education (BMCU) (2008). *Circular on the Education Sector's Assistance to Post- Sichuan Earthquake Reconstruction, 26 September 2008*. Available at: bjedu.gov.cn/publish/portal0/tab67/info8938.htm [Accessed 1 December 2011].

Bjnews (2008). 6,581 teachers and students perished and 1,274 missing in Sichuan Province in the earthquake, *Beijing News*, 24 May. Available at: news.21cn.com/zhuanti/domestic/08dizhen/2008/05/24/4759848.shtml [Accessed 1 December 2011].

BJSF (2011). *Beijing-Shifang Distance Education & Training Resources*. Online. Available at: bjsf.bjedu. cn [Accessed 1 December 2011].

BNU (2008a). *Psychological Support and Healing after Emergencies: Self-help Guidebook after the 5.12 Sichuan Earthquake*. Beijing: China Light Industry Press.

—(2008b). *Help the Children to Rebuild Psychological Home: Group Counselling Guidebook for Primary Schools*. Beijing: Beijing Normal University Press.

—(2008c). *Help the Children to Rebuild Psychological Home: Group Counselling Guidebook for Secondary Schools*. Beijing: Beijing Normal University Press.

China (2008). Wen Jibao: make schools into the safest public buildings. *China.com.cn*, 23 June. Available at: www.china.com.cn/news/txt/2008-06/23/content_15869723.htm [Accessed 1 December 2011].

China Economy (CE) Weekly (2008). 'Investigation said four times more school buildings than government buildings were destroyed in Sichuan earthquake', *China Economy Weekly*, 25 May. Available at: gongyi.people.com.cn/GB/151650/152509/9354470.html [Accessed 1 December 2011].

Deyang Daily (2011). 'Source of Mianzhu's education rebirth', *Dailyang Daily*, 9 May. Available at: deyang.scol.com.cn/qxxw/content/2011-05-09/content_51096926.htm?node=110558 [Accessed 1 December 2011].

Finance & Economy (2008). 'School collapsed due to poor quality'. *Finance & Economy*, 3 June. Available at: www.caijing.com.cn/2008-06-03/100067212.html [Accessed 1 December 2011].

FT China (2010). 'China Life Insurance provides support to all earthquake orphans'. *Financial Times China*, 22 April. Available at: news.xinhuanet.com/finance/2010-04/22/c_1249095.htm [Accessed 1 December 2011].

Gov.cn (2008a). 'Ten "firsts" that follow massive quake'. *GOV.cn*. Online, 13 June. Available at: english. gov.cn/2008-06/13/content_1015746.htm [Accessed 1 December 2011].

—(2008b). 'The State Council General Committee approved state guidelines on performance-based salaries for teachers in compulsory education', *GOV.cn*. Online, 21 December. Available at: www. gov.cn/ldhd/2008-12/21/content_1184109.htm [Accessed 1 December 2011].

—(2009). 'Official admits "possible quality problems" of school buildings damaged in Sichuan earthquake', *Gov.cn*. Online, 4 September. Available at: english.gov.cn/2008-09/04/content_1087290.htm [Accessed 1 December 2011].

Guangming Daily (2011). 'Complete restoration of education to the level of pre-earthquake period', *Guangming Daily*, 12 May. Available at: topics.gmw.cn/2011-05/12/content_1956957.htm [Accessed 1 December 2011].

Jiang, S. and Peng B. (2010). Conditions of teacher development in post-earthquake reconstruction: issues and recommendations, *Journal of Sichuan College of Education*, 10, 85–7.

Ma, X. and Feng, W (2008). Problems and strategies in disaster education in Chinese schools. *Research in Basic Education*, 11, 3–4.

Mianzhu Online (2011). Hope for tomorrow: an overview of rapid development of education in Minazhu in post-earthquake reconstruction, *Mianzhu Online*. Available at: www.mz.gov.cn/jkjyfc/ ShowArticle.asp?ArticleID=14335 [Accessed 1 December 2011].

Ministry of Civil Affairs, China (MCA) (2008). *Emergent Circular of the Ministry of Civil Affairs on One-to-One Cross-region Assistance Scheme for Quake-affected Areas in the Great Sichuan*

Earthquake, 23 May. Available at: www.mca.gov.cn/article//zwgk/tzl/200805/20080500015221. shtml [Accessed 1 December 2011].

Ministry of Education (MOE) (2008a). *Circular of Ministry of Education on Psychological Counselling for Primary and Secondary Schools in Quake-Affected Regions,* 23 July. Available at: www.moe.gov.cn/ publicfiles/business/htmlfiles/moe/moe_2431/201001/xxgk_81889.htmly [Accessed 1 December 2011].

—(2008b). *East China University Provided Teacher-Training Centred Cross-regional Assistance to Dujiangyan,* 5 September. Available at: www.moe.gov.cn/publicfiles/business/htmlfiles/moe/ s169/201004/84181.html [Accessed 1 December 2011].

—(2008c). *Circular of the MOE, the Ministry of Housing and Urban-Rural Development (MHURD), and National Development and Reform Commission on the State Guidelines on School Planning and Construction for Post-earthquake Reconstruction,* 24 October. Available at: www.moe.gov.cn/ publicfiles/business/htmlfiles/moe/moe_1892/201001/xxgk_77147.html [Accessed 1 December 2011].

—(2009a). *Safe School Project of China, Ministry of Education.* Available at: www.moe.edu.cn/business/ htmlfiles/moe/moe_2698/index.html [Accessed 1 December 2011].

—(2009b). *Circular of 11 Ministries on Three Supplementary Documents Including Action Plan for Safe School Project, Ministry of Education,* 24 June. Available at: www.sdedu.gov.cn/sdedu_ztxx/.../ P020090720357404675938.doc [Accessed 1 December 2011].

—(2009c). *The Education Sector's State Plan for Rapid Response to Public Emergencies Resulting from Natural Disasters,* September.

—(2010). *Tongji University Provided Five Types of Cross-regional Assistance to Quake-affected Areas,* 6 October 2010. Available at: www.moe.gov.cn/publicfiles/business/htmlfiles/moe/ s165/201006/90050.html [Accessed 1 December 2011].

—(2011). *The Project of 'Making Schools the Safest Place' has Completed 250 Million Square Meters of School Buildings,* May. Available at: www.moe.edu.cn/publicfiles/business/htmlfiles/moe/ moe_2899/201105/119082.html [Accessed 1 December 2011].

National Institute of Education Sciences (NIES) (2009). Mid-term report on post- 5.12 Wenchuan earthquake reconstruction research. *Education Sciences Forum,* 8, 48–51.

National Working Committee on Children and Women (NWCCW) (2009). *The Child Friendly Space Working Newsletter of April 2009, China's National Working Committee on Children and Women (NWCCW) and UNICEF, 2009 (4).*

People's Daily (2008). 'Beijing Normal University a hotline to provide psychological support and information services'. *People's Daily* 22 May. Available at: edu.people.com.cn/GB/7275921.html [Accessed 1 December 2011].

Quan, X. and Li, Y. (2011). Implications of Japanese disaster education for school education in China, *Journal of Teaching and Management,* 10, 87–8.

Science and Technology (ST) Daily (2011). 'Better schooling for children in quake-affected areas: three years of Beijing-Shifang twinning in education'. *Science & Technology Daily,* 12 May. Available at: www.stdaily.com/kjrb/content/2011-05/12/content_303993.htm [Accessed 1 December 2011].

Shanghai (2011). *Press Conference on Shanghai's Assistance to Post-earthquake Reconstruction in Dujiangyan,* Shanghai Municipal Government, 12 October. Available at: www.shanghai.gov.cn/ shanghai/node2314/node2319/node12344/u26ai28871.html [Accessed 1 December 2011].

Sichuan Daily (2011a). 'China children and teenagers' fund opened rehabilitation centres for Sichuan earthquake orphans and disabled children', *Sichuan Daily*, 31 August. Available at: society.scdaily.cn/ylws/content/2011-08/31/content_2786683.htm?node=3704 [Accessed 1 December 2011].

—(2011b). 'The Child Friendly Spaces successfully transited from emergency measures to permanent institutions', *Sichuan Daily*, 13 September. Available at: scwx.newssc.org/system/2011/09/13/013303062.shtml [Accessed 1 December 2011].

Sichuan News Agency (2008). 'Sichuan promised no child left behind from schools by the earthquake', *Sichuan News Agency*, 26 August. Available at: edu.people.com.cn/GB/1053/7728120.html [Accessed 1 December 2011].

Sichuan Online (2011). Child Friendly Spaces are praised as children's home for psychological recovery. *Sichuan Online*, 10 September. Available at: cbzx.scol.com.cn/cbzx1/content/2011-09/10/content_2830834.htm?node=177 [Accessed 1 December 2011].

Sina (2011). Beijing trained 3,000 Shifang teachers, and set up e-learning website. *Sina*, 17 May. Available at: gongyi.sina.com.cn/gyzx/2011-05-17/093826461.html [Accessed 1 December 2011].

State Council (2008a). *Circular of the State Council General Office on One-to-One Cross-region Assistance Scheme for Post –earthquake Recovery and Reconstruction, the State Council of People's Republic of China*, 18 June. Available at: www.gov.cn/zwgk/2008-06/18/content_1019966.htm [Accessed 1 December 2011].

—(2008b). *Circular of the State Council on the State Overall Planning for Post-Wenchuan Earthquake Restoration and Reconstruction, the State Council of People's Republic of China*, 23 September. Available at: www.gov.cn/zwgk/2008-09/23/content_1103686.htm [Accessed 1 December 2011].

—(2009). *China's Actions for Disaster Prevention and Reduction, the Information Office of the State Council, People's Republic of China*, 11 May. Available at: www.gov.cn/english/official/2009-05/11/content_1310629.htm [Accessed 1 December 2011].

Tan, X., Wang, M. and Zhang, Y. (2010). *International development trends in disaster education, Forum for Disaster Reduction*, 6, 8–10.

Tongji Urban Planning & Design Institute (TJUPDI) (2010). *Tongji Universities established two centres in Dujiangyan, Shanghai*, 29 December. Available at: www.tjupdi.com/website/news_detail.asp?id=1191 [Accessed 1 December 2011].

United Nations Children's Fund (UNICEF) (2009a). *Sichuan Earthquake: One-Year Report, Part One, May 2009*. Beijing; UNICEF Office for China. Available at: www.unicef.org/china/China_Earthquake_Report_2009ENG_Part_1.pdf [Accessed 8 December 2011].

—(2009b). *Sichuan Earthquake: One-Year Report, Part Two, May 2009*. Beijing: UNICEF Office for China. Available at: www.unicef.org/china/China_Earthquake_Report_2009ENG_Part_2.pdf [Accessed 8 December 2011].

—(2010). *Sichuan Earthquake: Two-Year Report, May 2010*. Beijing; UNICEF Office for China. Available at: www.unicef.org/china/Two_Year_Report_ENG_FINAL.pdf [Accessed 8 December 2011].

United Nations International Strategy for Disaster Reduction (UNISDR) (2011). *What is Disaster Risk Reduction?* Online. UNISDR. Available at: www.unisdr.org/who-we-are/what-is-drr [Accessed 1 December 2011].

Wang, M., Shi, H. and Zhang, Y. (2011). A survey of international public disaster education. *Life and Disaster*, 5, 25–7.

Xiang, H., Huang, X., Wang, R., Pu, S. and He, Y. (2008). Psychological interventions in Mianyang City after the Wenchuan earthquakes, *China Journal of Evidence-based Medicine*, 8, 11, 918–21.

Xinhua (2008a). '*Ministries of Finance and Education of China provided 50 million Yuan emergent education fund*'. Xinhua News Agency, 14 May. Available at: news.xinhuanet.com/newscenter/2008-05/14/content_8171440.htm [Accessed 1 December 2011].

—(2008b). '*40 Counties in Severely Affected Areas in Sichuan Postponed National College Entrace Examinations*'. Xinhua News Agency, 19 May. Available at: news.xinhuanet.com/edu/2008-05/19/content_8203421.htm [Accessed 1 December 2011].

—(2008c). '*Students in Secondary Vocational Schools Moved to Regions Across China to Resume Schooling*'. Xinhua News Agency, 25 May. Available at: big5.xinhuanet.com/gate/big5/news.xinhuanet.com/newscenter/2008-08/25/content_9709367.htm [Accessed 1 December 2011].

—(2008d). '*Universities and Colleges Administrated by the Ministry of Education Provided Emergency Subsidies to Students from Quake-affected Areas*'. Xinhua News Agency, 28 May. Available at: news.xinhuanet.com/newscenter/2008-05/28/content_8270013.htm [Accessed 1 December 2011].

—(2008e). '*About 3.4 Million Students in Sichuan Quake-affected Areas to Return to Schools on 1 September*'. Xinhua News Agency, 31 August. Available at: news.xinhuanet.com/newscenter/2008-08/31/content_9744735.htm [Accessed 1 December 2011].

—(2009a). '*School Reconstruction Proceeds Smoothly: Over 3,000 are Under Construction*'. Xinhua News Agency, 11 May. Available at: news.xinhuanet.com/newscenter/2009-05/11/content_11354961.htm [Accessed 1 December 2011].

—(2009b). '*5,335 Students Perished or Missing in Sichuan Province in the Earthquake*'. Xinhua News Agency, 7 May. Available at: news.xinhuanet.com/newscenter/2009-05/07/content_11328503.htm [Accessed 1 December 2011].

—(2011). '*Sichuan: Post-Earthquake School Reconstruction Completed 99%*'. Xinhua News Agency, 9 November. Available at: news.xinhuanet.com/2011-11/09/c_122257548.htm [Accessed 1 December 2011].

Xue, E. (2008). Strategic choices for education facing natural disaster: case studies of Japan, India and Iran. *Comparative Education Review*, 10, 76–80.

Zhang, C. (2008). A case study of the local government's response to post-earthquake education reconstruction in Hanwang Town, Mianzhu Prefecture, Sichuan Province after the 5.12 Sichuan earthquake: pathway and difficulties. *Time Education*, 9.

Zhang, Y. (2009). Cultural ecology of temporary schools in quake-affected areas. *Journal of the Chinese Society of Education*, 9.

Zhang, Y. and Wang, M. (2010). Prospects of disaster education in China. *City and Disaster Reduction*, 5, 10-13.

Zhang, Y., Wang, M. and Tan, X. (2011). Preliminary thoughts on research of disaster education theory and practice. *Journal of Catastrophology*, 26, 1, 109–17.

Earthquake, Tsunami and Nuclear Disaster in Japan: The Immediate Aftermath

Fumiaki Ema

Introduction

On 11 March 2011, a 9.0 Magnitude earthquake struck eastern Japan. As of 16 November 2011, the official death toll has reached 15,839, with a further 3,467 people still missing. The mortality figure exceeds the 6,434 people that died in the Great Hanshin-Awaji Earthquake of 1995, making what occurred in March 2011 the most devastating disaster in Japan since the end of World War II. The massive natural disaster completely transformed the landscape in affected areas. In the nine months that have since passed, the disaster has already led to the beginnings of a major review of previously accepted approaches to disaster preparation, response and recovery that had long been regarded as the norm in Japanese society. Among other things, the Great East Japan Earthquake has exposed problems regarding disaster prevention and energy use in post-war Japanese society. The contribution of this chapter will be to identify and examine some of the conditions faced by schools after the earthquake, based on interviews with teachers and other stakeholders who were affected by the earthquake. An attempt will then be made to identify educational issues for future disaster prevention and disaster mitigation at this time.

To achieve all of the above, the following structure will be adopted. The chapter will consider in turn: key characteristics of the Great East Japan Earthquake; the disaster culture of tsunamis and the role of education; the school context, with particular reference to reports from teachers in Ishinomaki; mental care issues; and the nuclear power plant disaster and implications for the role of disaster education. An attempt will then be made to draw some key conclusions.

As part of the research process, the writer of this chapter worked closely with schools in the three prefectures most affected by the earthquake – Iwate, Miyagi and Fukushima – over a nine-month period. Extensive interviews with teachers and other stakeholders were conducted. Some of the first-hand interview transcripts accumulated during this involvement will form an important part of the story to be told. However, before considering the experiences of the schools themselves, the first task that has been set is to provide a short overview of some of the characteristics of the Great East Japan Earthquake and examine these in relation to specific categories of hazard: earthquake; tsunami; and nuclear power plant catastrophe.

Characteristics of the Great East Japan Earthquake

The three prefectures most affected by the earthquake and tsunami were Iwate, Miyagi and Fukushima, as shown in the Map presented as Figure 7.1.

According to the National Police Agency, 12,143 (92.5%) of the 13,135 confirmed dead in these three prefectures were drowned. Compared to the Great Hanshin-Awaji Earthquake of 1995, when most of the dead were crushed by collapsing buildings, it can be seen that in the Great East Japan

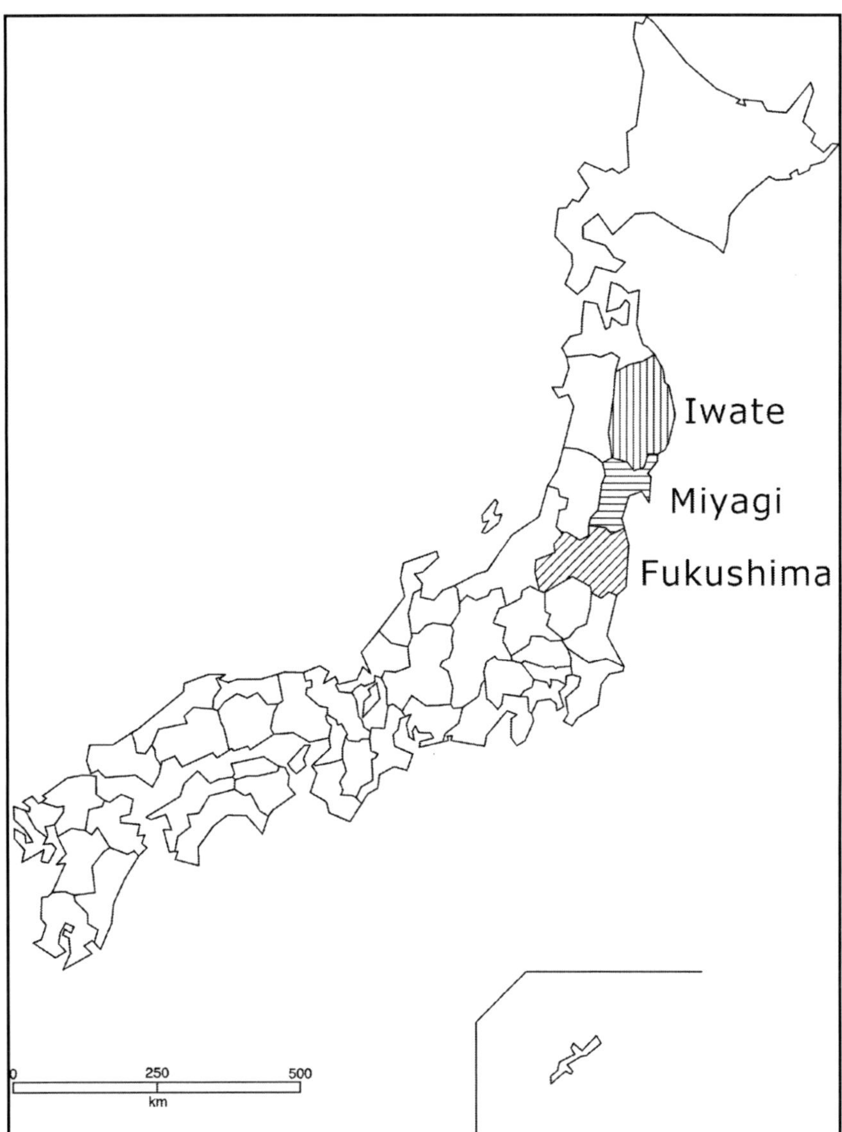

Figure 7.1 A Map Showing the Three Prefectures Most Affected by the Great East Japan Earthquake of 2011

Earthquake, most people were killed by the tsunami. Furthermore, according to this report, 65.2% of the people killed in the Great East Japan Earthquake were aged 60 or more. It is estimated that many of the elderly died when they were caught in the tsunami due to their inability to escape quickly after the earthquake (ADRC and IRP, 2011). The numbers of children and teachers killed in Iwate, Miyagi and Fukushima prefectures during the Great East Japan Earthquake, according to the Ministry of Education, Culture, Sports, Science and Technology, are detailed in Table 8.1 below.

Damage was most severe in Miyagi. In one elementary school, near the coast in Ishinomaki, 74 of the 108 school children died or are listed as missing as a result of the tsunami. In the same school, nine of the 11 teachers were killed.

One of the characteristics of the Great East Japan Earthquake is that the disaster was threefold due to the occurrence of the earthquake, the tsunami and the nuclear power plant accident. This characteristic is deeply entwined with the geographic and economic conditions in Japan. Geographically, the Japanese Archipelago is located on the Pacific Ring of Fire. The Japanese Archipelago only covers 0.25% of the earth's surface, but earthquake activity is frequent. There were 912 earthquakes of Magnitude 6 or higher between 1995 and 2005, and approximately 20% of these occurred in or around the Japanese Archipelago. Meanwhile, economically Japan is a developed country. Its industrial sector consumes an enormous amount of energy. Of the total amount of electric power Japan generated in 2009, 8% was hydro power; 62% thermal power; and 29% nuclear power. In 2011, there were 54 nuclear reactors used for power generation in the Japanese Archipelago. This is approximately 13% of the world's power reactors. The power generated by nuclear power plants in Fukushima is sent to the distant Tokyo metropolitan area to be consumed. Thus many nuclear power plants serving the rest of the country are located in the earthquake-susceptible Japanese Archipelago. Since the 1970s, numerous researchers

	Dead				Missing	Total
	Kindergarten children	Primary school children	Junior high and high school students	Teachers		
Iwate	10	17	62	8	27	124
Miyagi	65	166	152	22	56	461
Fukushima	4	24	50	3	10	91
Total	79	207	264	33	93	676

Source: Based on data abstracted from: Ministry of Education, Culture, Sports, Science and Technology, 2011a.

Table 8.1 Children and Teachers Killed and Missing in Three Prefectures Due to the Great East Japan Earthquake (as of 16 November 2011)

and local residents have repeatedly expressed concerns that these nuclear power plants would cause large-scale radiation harm if damaged in a major earthquake.

What occurred in March 2011 at the Fukushima Daiichi Nuclear Power Plant was as follows. Nuclear reactors that were in operation were shut down immediately after the earthquake. After shutdown, a nuclear reactor must be cooled. However, a giant tsunami engulfed the Fukushima Daiichi Nuclear Power Plant, destroying the power supply for sending cooling water. Because of this, problems occurred in the reactors, and the buildings housing Reactors 1 and 3 were blown away in hydrogen explosions. Cracking also occurred in Reactor 2, believed to be caused by a hydrogen explosion. As a result of all of this, a large amount of radioactive material was released outside the facility.

Half a year after the earthquake, the situation at Fukushima Daiichi Nuclear Power Plant is no longer quite so critical, as technical problems have come under increasing control. However, the area within a 20-kilometre radius of Fukushima Daiichi Nuclear Power Plant has been designated, and remains as, an exclusion zone. Approximately 78,000 residents have been forced to take refuge away from their homes. As of September 2011, 11,918 infants and students have been transferred from Fukushima to schools outside the prefecture. This is mainly because family members are concerned about the exposure of their children to radiation.

The Disaster Culture of Tsunamis and the Role of Education

The coastal area affected by the tsunami following the earthquake is known as the Sanriku Coast. Comprising 36 bays, likened to a 'saw tooth' ('ria') formation, this irregular coastline tends to amplify the destructiveness of tsunami waves. Cold and warm currents meet offshore of the Sanriku coast, making the area an abundant fishing ground. Perhaps not surprisingly, the main industries in the region are fisheries, fish farming and seafood processing. The Sanriku coastal region has been known as an area susceptible to tsunamis. The Meiji-Sanriku Tsunami of 1896 and the Showa Sanriku Tsunami of 1933 caused great damage to the region.

Consequently, over the years, passionate efforts have been made to understand better the nature and behaviour of tsunamis and to introduce remedial measures to reduce their impact. For instance, Kenji Yamazaki used the example of Taro on the Iwate coast to reveal some of the characteristics of disaster-prevention in the event of a tsunami (Yamazaki and Yamazaki, 2011). In the Taro earthquake and tsunami of 1896, only 36 of approximately 1,895 residents survived. When a similar disaster stuck again, in 1933, only 1820 of the 2731 residents survived. Consequently, from 1934 onwards, the residents of Taro began constructing dikes to protect the town from tsunamis. The construction of dikes continued, except for an interruption during the war, until the first phase of work was completed in 1958. The dikes that were put in place were 10 metres above sea level and 1,380 metres in length. Thanks to these dikes, Taro suffered no loss of life due to the tsunami caused by the Chile earthquake in 1960. Further construction continued after this. Before the 2011 earthquake, the dikes had reached a total length of 2,400 metres.

At the same time as creating infrastructure such as dikes, special effort was also given to passing along the experiences and lessons learned from tsunamis. The presence of dikes is both physically and psychologically reassuring. However, the most decisive thing in the event of a tsunami is for each person to escape quickly to high ground. This knowledge is referred to, in the Sanriku region, as *tsunami tendenko* (tsunami scatter). This means: 'When there is a tsunami, run to high ground. It is alright to separate from others. Just think about your own safety and don't worry about anyone else.' For example, Yoshi Tabata, who is a survivor of the 1933 tsunami, volunteered to tell her story for over 30 years using a picture-story show (Tabata, 2011). The absorption of stories of this kind, over the years, can be considered to have created a type of disaster culture. This 'culture' is used to pass on the disaster experiences of individuals and organizations in a comprehensive form in an effort to ensure appropriate mental responses and actions to prevent and mitigate disasters, and also to enhance the capacity of individuals, organizations and society to maintain functionality and adapt.

In ways of this kind, by 2011 the Sanriku region had built up infrastructure and focused on passing along disaster experiences in order to reduce the damage caused by tsunamis. However, responding through infrastructure has limitations. The tsunami caused by the Great East Japan Earthquake was, in many locations, 14 or 15 metres high. In Taro itself, the tsunami exceeded 20 metres in height and flowed over the dikes into the town. At its highest point – in Miyako, Iwate – the tsunami was 38.9 metres. Moreover, on the Sendai Plain, which has a flat coastal area, the tsunami reached 5.5 kilometres inland from the coastline.

Faced with such an enormous tsunami, it is vital to try to consider and learn from the following question: what points of disaster education and training in schools worked well and what points did not? An attempt will now be made to do just this, by focusing on primary schools and junior high schools in Ishinomaki, most affected by the earthquake.

Reports from Teachers in Ishinomaki

With a population of 162,000, Ishinomaki is the second largest city in Miyagi prefecture. It is the city where children and teachers were most affected by the earthquake: 29 kindergarten children, 125 primary school children, 56 junior high and high school students and 12 teachers were killed. There are 43 primary schools and 21 junior high schools in Ishinomaki. The damage to municipal primary and junior high schools can be classified into three types as detailed in Table 8.2 below.

An example from each of Type II and Type III schools will now be examined with regard to the subsequent restoration process.

A Type III Primary School

Ogatsu Primary School is located at the back of a 'ria' coastline bay. It suffered Type III damage. A 5th-Grade teacher from this primary school described the disaster as follows:

> The children were cleaning the classroom. I was in the staffroom preparing handouts for the children. Then it happened. The shaking threw me into the air. I ran from the staffroom up to the second floor to the 5th Grade classroom. The children were cowering beneath the desks at the back of the room. I called out their names and confirmed that they were all present. The shaking still continued throughout this period. The manual says to guide the children according to the announcements made throughout the school. However, there was no communication. I kept telling two nearby girls who were crying that it would be all right. When the shaking stopped, I took the children out into the schoolyard. The

	No damage (Type I)	Partial damage or inundation above floor level (Type II)	First floor submerged or complete destruction of facility (Type III)	Total
Elementary schools	7 (16%)	26 (61%)	10 (23%)	43
Junior high schools	9 (43%)	8 (38%)	4 (19%)	21

Source: based on data abstracted from: Ishinomaki City, 2011.

Table 8.2 Damage to Ishinomaki Municipal Primary and Junior High Schools

> corridors were filled with shattered glass. Once I had confirmed the evacuation of the children, I handed over the children to their parents who had come to pick them up.
>
> (Interview with male; 37 years old)

This episode can be used to indicate the appropriate action to take after the occurrence of an earthquake. During the shaking caused by the earthquake, the children took refuge under desks of their own accord despite the teacher not being present. The evacuation to the schoolyard was also conducted swiftly. It can be seen that training regarding appropriate disaster-evacuation behaviour, carried out on an everyday basis, had indeed shaped the response that actually occurred. The teacher also had a strong sense of responsibility over the lives of the children and provided comfort to them. If the disaster ended then, it would have been no more than a large earthquake. But what then occurred, in March 2011, was the onslaught of the tsunami:

> The tsunami alarm began to sound shortly afterwards. Due to the experience of the 1960 Chile earthquake and tsunami, there were documents and stone markers indicating that ships had been pushed as far as the schoolyard, and it was thus believed that a tsunami would not reach any higher than the schoolyard. It was also snowing, so it was also suggested that we evacuate to the gymnasium, but we decided to take refuge in a shrine on high ground behind the school. 'If a tsunami comes, run for the hills' is something local residents constantly mentioned. Several children were also handed over to their parents at the shrine on the hill.
>
> The cries of 'It's a tsunami! Get to high ground!' and the sound of houses and power poles being destroyed drew nearer as the tsunami approached along the road that runs straight through the centre of town. We did our best to climb the narrow path that led to the summit. We told the children to look straight ahead as they walked to prevent them from seeing the tsunami. A local elderly woman who could no longer walk was carried by two teachers. There were fallen trees along the way, but with the help of the local residents, we were able to reach the summit.
>
> (Ibid.)

The above account can be used to reveal the dualistic nature that tsunami experiences can have in terms of impacting upon behaviour. On the one hand, tsunami experiences function for mitigating disaster. In this case, use of the wisdom 'If a tsunami comes, run for the hills' was crucial to survival. The height of the tsunami exceeded that of the roof of Ogatsu Primary School. If the children and teachers had taken refuge in the gymnasium or on the roof of the school building, many lives would have been lost. This wisdom is a disaster culture passed along in society, i.e. the aforementioned *tsunami tendenko*. On the other hand, previous experience of tsunamis may confuse decisions about evacuating. In particular, the experience of the Chile earthquake and tsunami created the judgement that 'the tsunami won't come this far' and many people were caught up in the tsunami as a result. A tendency to view the danger of a disaster lightly and not take appropriate actions has been termed a 'normalcy bias'. Past tsunami experience may amplify this bias. In the disaster of March 2011, people who first took refuge in an evacuation centre and then climbed hills, because they thought they were in danger, survived. Making one's own decision to escape to a safer location is at the core of the disaster culture surrounding tsunamis. The children and teachers of Ogatsu Primary School, along with the local residents, subsequently fled from the summit where they had taken refuge. This represents the next episode:

> The fire department suggested that we leave the summit where we had taken refuge and walk further to take shelter in a waste disposal plant behind the hill. It continued to snow and we were surrounded by darkness. Even the kindergarten children who were woken from their midday naps to take refuge walked in their pyjamas without crying.
>
> At the waste disposal plant, while it was still light, we made a list of the children that had taken refuge. We used cardboard to create bedding on the floor. Then, we told the children that they couldn't go home and that there was nothing to eat. None of the children complained of being hungry that night. Because we were in a waste disposal plant, we had no trouble finding things to burn, but it was a cold night. Outside the plant, we stood around fires and exchanged information with the local residents. Our means of communication had been lost in the tsunami, and we spent the night filled with concerns. The children who couldn't sleep were singing the songs that we had planned to sing at the graduation ceremony the following week. They comforted each other while singing the songs.
>
> When we went down the hill the following day to collect information, the town had been destroyed. It was like looking at photos of the aftermath of a nuclear bomb. I joined several others to walk to the City Office in order to get food delivered. Walking was the only option now that cars and mobile phones had been washed away.
>
> About a month after the earthquake, Ogatsu Primary School began the new school year by borrowing the school building of a junior high school in a neighbouring area.
>
> (Ibid.)

The above account demonstrates how children and adults helped each other to deal with the disaster. Teachers and local residents worked together, and children comforted each other. This degree of order and mutual support was crucial in helping everyone to work together to overcome the disaster.

A Type II Junior High School

Yamashita Junior High School is located in the centre of Ishinomaki City, around two kilometres from the coastline. A teacher from this junior high school described the disaster as follows:

> Yamashita Junior High School was an earthquake-proof building, so there was no damage from the quake. After the shaking stopped, there was a tsunami warning for 'a tsunami over 3 metres high.' The school was two kilometres from the coastline, so we believed that even if the tsunami reached us, it would just be a few centimetres high by then and only cover our feet. However, the tsunami was actually much larger (some witnesses have said 12 metres). The canal to the port, located to the north of the school building, overflowed due to backflow from the tsunami. The first floor of the school building was covered by about 20 centimetres of water. The school building stood alone, surrounded by water. The students were evacuated to the third and fourth floors. Around 160 people remained in the building, including 94 students, 50 local residents who had taken refuge, as well as teachers.
>
> (Interview with male; 54 years old)

Japan has been systematically 'quake-proofing' school buildings. 103.2 billion yen was spent for this purpose in the fiscal year 2010 alone. According to April 2011 figures, the proportion of earthquake-proofed elementary and junior high school buildings had reached 80.3%. Yamashita Junior High School was not damaged by the shaking caused by the earthquake. However, measures to address tsunamis had been delayed. Furthermore, because the school was located inland, tsunamis had not been addressed in this particular school's disaster plan. The initial communication of a 'tsunami more than three metres high' also led to underestimation of the tsunami.

Further exacerbating what actually occurred, the school became isolated as an evacuation centre:

> Yamashita Junior High School had been designated as a disaster evacuation centre, but there was only enough food and blankets for 100 people. The stoves were on the first floor and couldn't be used due to being exposed to water. Classroom curtains were removed to use as blankets, and the alcohol lamps in the science lab were used to boil water. It was a cold night. Fires had broken out in the neighbouring houses, and we spent the night filled with concern. The following

day, the Self-Defence Forces came to rescue us from the building. We moved to the evacuation centre in a nearby primary school that was not damaged.

(Ibid.)

In Japan, many school buildings have been designated as evacuation centres. When a disaster first occurs, teachers often handle the operation of such centres. At Yamashita Junior High School, priority was given to students and local residents when handing out food and blankets, and there were not enough for the teachers. The teachers were also victims, but they dealt with the disaster with a strong sense of responsibility in carrying out their duties. The assistant headteacher of the school told this writer that, although the number of people remaining in the school building exceeded the disaster plan, it managed to function as an evacuation centre because it needed to do so for only one day. He then explained what happened next, as far as he was concerned, and what he observed and experienced:

> From the day after the earthquake, until March 23, I myself stayed at an evacuation centre in a primary school with 90 students. There were no bathing facilities. Teachers sought to confirm that students were safe by wandering around neighbouring evacuation centres. Students gradually began to be handed over to their parents when they could be contacted. During this period, junior high school students focused on cleaning the toilets in the evacuation centre, in addition to sorting and handing out relief supplies. They also worked with local residents to handle part of the operation of the evacuation centre. The students were also relied upon by the local residents who told them, 'You are doing a great job. Thank you.' Even after leaving the evacuation centre to return to their families, the junior high school students took the initiative to help out when relief supplies were delivered to the area and take them to the homes of the elderly in the community who were unable to walk.

(Ibid.)

Several research studies have indicated that actually carrying out roles suitable for their age to overcome difficult conditions after a disaster can be effective for the mental recovery of children (see, for example: Raphael, 1986; and Kato and Saisho, 2011). In the context described above, junior high school students found suitable roles for themselves and took action. Being relied upon by the people around them enabled them to face the disaster with their own strength. Teachers have indicated that it is important for junior high school students to experience working with local residents to help each other, not only in disasters but also on an everyday basis.

To continue the story:

> On 26 March, teachers entered the Yamashita Junior High School Building affected by the disaster and began cleaning the mud from the floors. Volunteers from outside the prefecture also helped a lot. For example, around 60 students from the Maiko High School Environment and Disaster Mitigation Course in Hyogo prefecture came for three days. They helped clean up the debris and mud. We were at a loss doing it ourselves. We really felt grateful for the increased number of people. The mud that covered the school ground was scooped up by the Self Defence Forces and the US military using heavy machinery. The new semester began on April 21, and the students returned to school.
>
> (Ibid.)

Much debris and mud remained in Ishinomaki after the tsunami. The only way to remove the mud from the school building was to clean it by hand. This was done by volunteers. NGOs and local groups in Ishinomaki worked together to accept volunteers, and a total of 100,000 people worked on recovery efforts in the seven months after the earthquake. Maiko High School in Hyogo prefecture is a high school that created a dedicated Environment and Disaster Mitigation Course after the Great Hanshin-Awaji Earthquake (Suwa, 2009). Students took turns to participate in volunteer activities to assist areas affected by the disaster.

Mental Care Issues

Nine months have passed since the earthquake occurred. What are the issues currently faced in schools? The teachers in Ishinomaki say that they are paying priority attention to 'mental care'. The term 'mental care' refers here to a variety of psychological support for people who have suffered trauma in disasters or major accidents. A common thread in the schools in Ishinomaki is that much attention is being given to how children have changed.

Primary school students and junior high school students apparently started school life calmly when school activities were reinstated just over a month after the earthquake. Compared to before the earthquake, there was greater discipline and students appeared to be concentrating on learning. According to Raphael (1986), after the impact phase of a disaster, there is a 'honeymoon phase' when people are altruistic and mutually supportive in the period immediately after suffering a disaster. A sense of working together to overcome the disaster can be seen among people. The initial behaviour of the children at school in Ishinomaki can thus be seen as a manifestation of this 'honeymoon phase'. One primary school teacher said the following.

> For about six months after the earthquake, I felt that there were many 'well-behaved' children. I think there were many instances in which the children had to be patient because of the curse of 'let's try hard'. There were few negative comments such as 'It's too hard' or 'It's too tough' and sometimes the children did not seem very childlike.
>
> (Interview with male; 38 years old)

However, the stress of the earthquake began to appear after some time. For example, the following reports were received in September:

- Junior high school students being frightened by loud noises or the ongoing aftershocks;
- Primary school students complaining of difficulty sleeping or irritability (unidentified complaints);
- Junior high school students suffering panic attacks when reminded of the earthquake by the waves and shaking of attractions at amusement parks.

To address these issues, schools have increased the numbers of nursing teachers and school counsellors, providing a stronger framework for responding to inquiries from children. According to a June 2011 announcement by the Ministry of Education, Culture, Sports, Science and Technology, 1,080 new teachers were assigned as a result of the earthquake. Of these, 244 were assigned to Miyagi, 235 to Iwate and 514 to Fukushima, which were the three prefectures most severely affected by the disaster.

Teachers want to bring about children's recovery from mental suffering by ensuring the children's lives are safe and stable. However, the tsunami destroyed the seafood processing plants and other industrial activity in the area, resulting in parents losing their jobs and instability in some families. Many such families have needed, or will need, to move to other areas in search of work. This is a cause of stress for children. Restoration of the local community is a condition required for the recovery of children.

It is now appropriate to turn to an examination of the nuclear power plant accident, and with particular reference to an educational perspective. This was a development that became such an important aspect of the overall disaster.

The Nuclear Power Plant Disaster and Education

Japan suffered atomic bombing in World War II. The people of Japan are thus particularly sensitive to nuclear power plant accidents and disasters based on memory of Hiroshima and Nagasaki. The notion that 'radiation is frightening' is widely shared among the people. However, nuclear power plant accidents are not experienced as frequently as earthquakes and tsunamis. Because of this, no disaster culture for mitigating nuclear power plant disasters has formed in the way that has occurred for earthquakes and tsunamis. It is known that accidents related to nuclear power cause enormous damage once they occur. However, it is difficult to envisage specific ways of reducing the damage.

It has been confirmed that Fukushima Daiichi Nuclear Power Plant suffered meltdowns of reactor cores. At the time of writing, engineers are continuing to work to bring about a cold shutdown of the reactors. The area within a 20-kilometre radius of the power plant has been designated as an 'exclusion zone' and entry is prohibited. According to the Ministry of Education, Culture, Sports, Science and Technology, radioactive material emitted from the Fukushima Daiichi Nuclear Power Plant has accumulated in 13 prefectures. This is approximately 8% of the land in Japan (Ministry of Education, Culture, Sports, Science and Technology, 2011b). Radiation levels are continually being monitored in various regions, centred on the area affected by the disaster. The radiation levels have decreased significantly compared to immediately after the disaster. Furthermore, progress is being made to remove nuclear contamination in each region, using annual exposure of 'one millisievert' (mSv: a measure of the absorption of radiation by the human body) as a yardstick.

Meanwhile, the social, psychological and economic damage caused by the Fukushima nuclear power plant accident has been profound. Over 10,000 children have transferred from schools within Fukushima to schools outside the prefecture. Comments such as 'Women from Fukushima can't get married' have been made on the internet, inflicting psychological damage on the victims of the disaster. It has also been reported that harmful rumours have caused damage, due to consumers avoiding agricultural products and seafood from areas affected by the nuclear power plant accident. Even if such products are scientifically proven to be safe, the damage cause by such harmful rumours is expected to be prolonged.

Radioactivity and radiation differ from other hazards, and the disasters that they can cause, in that they cannot be seen or heard. Specialized equipment is required for detection, and specialized knowledge is used to interpret the detected data. Because of this, many residents feel that 'Radiation is scary because you can't see it and much is unknown because there is a mixture of information and varied assessments.' School education, particularly in natural science, is necessary for providing students with the correct knowledge and judgement concerning radioactivity and radiation.

Nuclear Energy and Disaster Education

The Fukushima nuclear power plant accident has sparked discussion questioning Japan's dependence on nuclear power. Since the earthquake, several junior high school and high school teachers have reported conducting social studies lessons thinking about whether Japan should continue to use nuclear power generation in the future. For example, according to a report from one high school teacher, of 180 high school students, 26% said Japan should continue using nuclear power in the same way as now; 26% said Japan should cease using nuclear power; and 41% said that Japan should reduce the use of nuclear power as it switched to alternative energy sources (Kawaguchi, 2011). Many high school students believe that nuclear power is necessary and cannot be eliminated.

Where does this awareness come from? One cause is the content of social studies textbooks. For example, one of the junior high school social studies textbooks used in the past decade describes nuclear power as follows:

> Burning fossil fuels such as coal, oil and gas, emits carbon dioxide, which causes global warming. Nuclear power, which emits almost no carbon dioxide, was developed as an alternative energy source to replace fossil fuels. It currently accounts for approximately 30% of the power produced in Japan. However, there are issues concerning the safety of nuclear power. Once an accident occurs, the damage can be serious and irreparable. Even without accidents, there is also the issue of spent fuel (radioactive material). Many believe that a cautious approach including abolition is required.
>
> (Kyoiku-Shuppan, 2001)

This example can perhaps be considered as typical, in that Japanese social studies textbooks tend to be written with a balance of affirmative and opposing opinions concerning social issues. However, since the Kyoto Protocol was enacted in 1997, global warming and reducing emissions of carbon dioxide have become central themes concerning the global environment. Admittedly, nuclear power emits less carbon dioxide than fossil fuels during operation. If this point is emphasized, readers of textbooks are likely to be conscious that nuclear power is an energy source that must be used. It is believed that the view of high school students, that nuclear power is necessary, is supported by making this connection to the issue of the global environment.

However, the Fukushima nuclear power plant accident has prompted a review of the approach that nuclear power is necessary. It is becoming increasingly recognised that the damage to the environment and the energy required for restoration are enormous, once an accident occurs in a nuclear power plant. Thus the philosophy of 'sustainability' must be reconsidered. Is it really necessary to continue relying upon nuclear power, as in the past, despite being aware of the risks for Japanese society to continue to develop in the future? Or should we reduce the amount of energy used, while making the transition to renewable energy sources such as wind and solar power? It could be said that it is questions of this kind that the disaster has asked of Japanese society. Education has many roles to play in informing and stimulating the debate and in finding solutions.

Conclusion

Three particular points concerning future disaster prevention and disaster mitigation, emerging from the discussion above, are worth highlighting by way of conclusion. The first relates to the content of education for mitigating the effects of tsunamis. There are limitations on what can be achieved through infrastructure in disaster mitigation, and this needs to be complemented by appropriate education programs. In particular, it is important to appreciate that passing along tsunami experiences may work in a positive or a negative direction in affecting disaster mitigation. To ensure that exploiting the tradition of previous tsunami experiences and understanding, generated from events of this kind, work in the way intended, it is also necessary to take into account scientific knowledge such as 'normalcy bias' to ensure that children still appreciate the importance of making their own decisions.

The second point concerns the importance of linking schools and communities in the context of disaster prevention and disaster mitigation. During a disaster, and again during the recovery period, the community plays a vital role in many ways, from the operation of evacuation centres, to supporting the mental recovery of children. One conceivable approach, further to strengthen school-community relationships, is the joint implementation of disaster-related training by children and local residents.

A third and final key point emerging from the discussion above is the argued need for a comprehensive review of the content of formal school education from the perspective of disasters. In particular, the content of textbooks should be re-examined and especially with regards to value judgements about the necessity or otherwise of nuclear energy, and taking into account lessons from the nuclear power plant accident. Among other things, this means reviewing the school curriculum based on the idea of 'sustainability'.

Questions for Further Consideration

1. What lessons of relevance for other countries emerge from discussion of what happened in Japan in 2011, and the immediate aftermath period?
2. This chapter has focused on formal education and schooling in particular. What other lessons do you think emerge for informal education and the role of media?

Suggestions for Further Reading

1. One of the most recent reports to emerge in the aftermath period is: Government of Japan (2011). *Towards Reconstruction: Hope Beyond the Disaster*. Tokyo: Government of Japan. A provisional translation, in English, is now available at: www.cas.go.jp/jp/fukkou/english/pdf/report20110625.pdf [Accessed 20 December 2011]. The report provides guidelines for deciding what should be rebuilt and where. Particular emphasis is placed on the concept of 'disaster reduction' within the reconstruction process.
2. To keep abreast of emerging news related to the Great East Japan Earthquake of 2011, an excellent source is a dedicated web page set up for this purpose within the *PreventionWeb* portal: *Great East Japan Earthquake 2011*. Online. Available at: www.preventionweb.net/english/professional/news/tags/index.php/pw:jpnearthquake2011/Great%20East%20Japan%20Earthquake%202011/ [Accessed 20 December 2011].

References

Asian Disaster Reduction Centre (ADRC), International Recovery Platform (IRP) (2011). *Great East Japan Earthquake: Preliminary Observations*. Kobe: ADRC and IRP. Available at: www.adrc.asia/documents/disaster_info/2011March11_EastJapan_EarthquakeReport_%20final.pdf [Accessed 11 November 2011].

Ishinomaki City (2011). *Ishinomaki-shi Shiritsu Gakko Shisetsu Higai Jokyo* [Damage Report on Ishinomaki City Municipal School Facilities]. Ishinomaki: Board of Education. Available at: www.city.ishinomaki.lg.jp/kyouiku/link_2_3_2_2.jsp [Accessed 20 November 2011]. (Japanese).

Kato, H. and Saisho, H. (2011). *Kokoro no Kea – Hanshin-Awaji Daishinsai kara Tohoku e* [Mental Care – From the Great Hanshin-Awaji Earthquake to Tohoku], Kodansha. (Japanese).

Kawaguchi, Y. (2011). Yureru! Gempatsu Taio to Kokosei – Media Riterashii kara Gempatsu wo Otte [Shake! Dealing with nuclear power and high school students- following nuclear power through media literacy], *Rekishi Chiri Kyoiku*, 781, 60–3. (Japanese).

Kyoiku-Shuppan (2011). *Chugaku Shakai – Komin – Tomo ni Ikiru* [*Junior High School Social Studies – Civics – Living Together*] (Japanese).

Ministry of Education, Culture, Sports, Science and Technology (2011a). *Higashi-Nihon Daishinsai ni yoru Higai Jokyo ni Tsuite* [*Information on Damage Caused by the Great East Japan Earthquake*] (No. 170), Available at: www.mext.go.jp/component/a_menu/other/detail/__icsFiles/afieldfile/2011/11/24/135089_112410_1.pdf [Accessed 16 November 2011]. (Japanese).

—(2011b). *Hoshasenryo-to Bumpu Mappu* [*Map of Distribution of Radiation*], Available at: ramap.jaea.go.jp/map/mapdf/agreement.html [Accessed 20 November 2011].

Raphael, B. (1986). *When Disaster Strikes: How Individuals and Communities Cope with Catastrophe*. New York: Basic Books.

Suwa, S. (2009). *Disaster Mitigation Education: Present Situations and Problems: Maiko High School Environment and Disaster Mitigation*. Online. Available at: www.hyogo-c.ed.jp/~maiko-hs/e/DM_edu/psap/psap01.htm [Accessed 23 November 2011].

Tabata, Y. (2011). *Tsunami* [Passing on a tsunami experience to children – A picture story show, translated in English by Yamazaki,T.] Sankei Shinbun Shuppan.

Yamazaki, K. and Yamazaki, T. (2011). 'Tsunami Disasters in Seenigama Village, Sri Lanka, and Taro Town Town, Japan'. In: P. P. Karan and S. P. Subbian, eds. *The Indian Ocean Tsunami: The Global Response to a Natural Disaster*. Lexington: University Press of Kentucky, 135–59.

Conclusion
David Smawfield

'Education and Natural Disasters' is an extremely broad subject canvas. It is hoped the reader feels this volume has not only demonstrated this, but has also done justice to the area of study, in the context of a series on education as a humanitarian response. Consequently it is arguably an impossible task to try to tease out, by way of a short general conclusion, a few key summary points, from a diverse range of chapters, that could be considered both representative and relevant for all readers. This is especially the case when it is considered that what might have stood out for an engineer – say, on design of school buildings – is likely to be different for a psychologist more concerned with trauma. Furthermore, a policy-maker will be looking for different conclusions, lessons and guidance as compared, say, to a teacher or research student.

In my role as editor, to try to arrive at a few key pointers that could perhaps be considered fundamental, I asked all contributors to propose just two key points that they would like their readers to take away from their contributions as a means of building an overall summary. The result remains personal, and may not be representative of the subject as a whole, but a thought-provoking list nevertheless emerges. It is as follows:

- The challenge further to build institutional capacity, especially through transfer of know-how and through support from advanced institutions to less advanced institutions and regions (internationally and intra-nationally). Zhou Zhong's chapter on China has described extraordinary achievement in this regard, showing what can be possible [Smawfield].
- The important role that networks play. The contribution that *PreventionWeb* makes is a great achievement, but there is a challenge to do more [Smawfield].
- The importance of heeding the distinctions, and appreciating attendant implications, between: 'information dissemination' and 'education'; and also 'education to create awareness' and 'education to change behaviours' [Burns].
- Population diversity clearly calls for a range of educational approaches, in both formal and non-formal programmes, based on evaluations of existing programmes to highlight what type of education is most effective in conveying

safety messages and motivating individuals and groups to take appropriate preventative action [Burns].

- Education and natural disasters, if this topic is to be taken more seriously and have more impact, needs to be mainstreamed into national and development planning. It must not remain a peripheral activity [Bangay].
- The threat and reality of anthromorphic climate change cannot be over-estimated and has huge implications for education and natural disasters, now and in the future, including why this needs to be prioritised. [Bangay].
- The presence of capable individuals matters and this underscores the importance of academic and other programmes with DDR specialisms and themes. Whether in the design of schools or in the response to disaster, the presence of qualified practitioners can mitigate the potential for harm done to children [Newton].
- Not all responses to natural disasters can be the same and it is important to keep in mind the limitations of what might be generalizable and why. The discipline of Comparative Education has much to contribute in this regard [Newton].
- Strong schools are communities in themselves and it is this community spirit that is one of the most precious things that can be destroyed in a disaster. It is also the strength that can enable schools to pull through [Beaton and Ledgard].
- Leadership, team work and media savviness can be vital ingredients in helping schools to respond to and recover from natural disasters [Beaton and Ledgard].
- Disaster response creates an opportunity to build back more strongly and better [Zhong].
- There is a wealth of best practice responses and approaches in natural disaster contexts that can be learned from, adapted and used in mainstream policy and practice, in order better to promote increased education quality and socio-economic development [Zhong].
- It is important to link schools and their wider communities in the context of disaster prevention and disaster mitigation. During a disaster, and again during the recovery period, the wider community plays a vital role in many ways, from the operation of evacuation centres, to supporting the mental recovery of children [Ema].
- The nuclear disaster in Japan raises issues about what school textbooks say about nuclear energy and especially any value judgements conveyed about safety, the clean nature of the energy source and environmental sustainability [Ema].

What also comes across through the content of this volume is that 'Education and Natural Disasters' is a subject area in which there are huge achievements, know-how and resources to celebrate. The extensive references that have been provided and suggestions for further reading are a means to access such material. It is hoped, too, that this volume has contributed to building knowledge and awareness of quite what there is to be found, stimulated further interest, and promoted knowledge dissemination.

To be consistent with the rest of the book, it also seems appropriate to conclude with some final guiding questions.

Questions for Further Consideration

1. In the bulleted list above, what key points need to remain as separate and discrete considerations and where do you see possibilities for overlap, synergies and mutual reinforcement to create multiplier effects?
2. What have you taken away from reading this volume and what conclusions and lessons would you prioritise?